Angels Watching

MEMOIRS OF A COUNTRY GIRL FROM WAKARUSA

Shirley Gall McMillan

authorHOUSE®

AuthorHouse™
1663 Liberty Drive, Suite 200
Bloomington, IN 47403
www.authorhouse.com
Phone: 1-800-839-8640

First published by AuthorHouse 10/29/2007

ISBN: 978-1-4343-3503-6 (sc)

Printed in the United States of America
Bloomington, Indiana

This book is printed on acid-free paper.

For my son, Jimmy,

My granddaughters, Ashli and Chelsea,

My great-grandson, Camden,

And for great-grandchildren yet unborn.

Table of Contents

Part 2

LAUNCHING OUT

Part 3
MOVING ON

Dysfunctional Was Normal

Dysfunctional was normal in our family, but we didn't know it. In our family, normal meant sarcasm, criticism, put-downs, teasing, tormenting, belittling, insults, dismissing others' thoughts and feelings, secrets, don't-talk-about-it-and-it-will-go-away.

This book is intended to be a lighthearted and (mostly) honest look at the family I grew up in. It is not a tell-all book, for no single book could contain it all. Rather, this look at my life and memories will attempt to show the grace of God at work in the life of a young girl and her family, the woman she became, and who she is now as a senior citizen.

This book is about life as I experienced and perceived it. Other family members will remember the same events from different points of view. They could write volumes of their own. This is my book, and these are my memories.

My memories include growing up poor in a large family during the Depression and World War II. As the eldest child, I knew that our parents struggled to provide the bare necessities during those hard times. Yet, as a child, I could not begin to comprehend the intensity of their struggles or the enormity of the responsibility they felt.

Our parents were not perfect, but they did the best they could with what life handed them. They married too young, and had so many children they didn't know what to do. But they did marry, and they stayed married, and they managed to survive and provide for us through incredibly hard times. I honor them for that. Their faithfulness and determination, their hard work and sacrifices, their honor and integrity, and their devotion to each other and to us are qualities worthy of emulation.

Shirley McMillan
June 2007

PART 1

Growing Up

We were poor and we knew it.

⇒ 1 ⇐

An Amish Girl and an English Boy

Nora Miller was feeling quite grownup the summer of 1927. At fifteen, she had just finished eighth grade at Hepton, a one-room country school south of Nappanee, Indiana, and was ready to launch out on her own.

Though Nora was a bright student and loved school, she had no illusions about attending high school. Eighth grade was as far as Amish young people were allowed to go. After eighth grade a girl stayed home to help her parents with the never-ending work of running the farm and home, and often a cottage industry. Or she hired out to a family needing household help. Her destiny in life was to marry, have babies and raise a family.

Nora had already worked as a live-in hired girl during previous summers and sometimes during the school year. Now her family had moved again, to a house near the "pontoon" bridge in the Gravelton area east of Nappanee, and Nora was working for a nearby family.

That summer she met Babe Gall, a tall good-looking young buck with sandy red hair and hazel eyes. Babe was helping his grandparents, Frank and Anna Mitchell, who also lived near the pontoon bridge. Babe, whose real name was Thurlo, had turned seventeen in March. He had finished his junior year at Nappanee High School, but wasn't sure he wanted to go back for his senior year. He had other things on his mind that summer, especially after meeting that pretty Amish girl named Nora.

Nora's brown eyes danced and sparkled, and her dark brown hair glistened in the August sunshine. She stood five feet two inches tall, and Babe thought she was the cutest girl he'd ever met. He couldn't take his eyes off her.

At nearly six feet, Babe towered above Nora, and she liked that. Most of the men in her family—her dad and seven brothers—were small and wiry. It felt good to look up to a man. Way up. She liked Babe's jovial sense of humor, his boisterous laugh, his penchant for mimicry, and his playful teasing. She was used to teasing from her brothers, but this was a different kind of teasing, and she liked it.

Babe and Nora began keeping company right away, making arrangements to see each other as often as possible. When they were together Nora donned "English" clothes, loosened her dark tresses and left her prayer cap and bonnet at home.

Nora's parents, Ed and Amanda, hoped her little fling with the English boy would end soon and she would return to the Amish way of life. In the Amish tradition, young people in their late teens enjoy a period of freedom called "running around" before marrying and settling down to raise a family. During this time, usually two or three years, a young person can decide whether to remain in the Amish faith or adopt the freer "English" lifestyle. If she or he decides to stay, the next step is baptism and joining the Amish Church. By this time a young person has been keeping company with a prospective mate and they will soon be ready to announce their intention to marry.

At fifteen, Nora had already decided she would not join the Amish Church. She wanted to be free of Amish rules and restrictions, free to wear bright colors and pretty clothes, free to ride in automobiles and have fun. She was ready to leave the plain life of the Amish and adopt the "fancy" life of the wider community.

In October Nora found out she was pregnant. Neither she nor Babe had planned on that happening, but Nora assumed they would get married. Babe, on the other hand, wasn't ready to be a husband and father. He couldn't undo the father part, but he needed time to think about the marriage part. He needed to get away from it all and sort it out in his mind.

When he returned home a few weeks later, he still didn't know what to do. He was only seventeen and had no job or job skills. How could he support a wife and baby? How could he marry a girl who was only fifteen? Would her parents give their permission? Or would they shun both of them for the sin they had committed?

When Ed and Amanda moved to Wolf Lake, some twenty-five miles away, Nora moved in with the Gall family to await the birth of her child. Frank and Viola Gall lived in an apartment above a business on South Main Street in downtown Nappanee. It was a full house, with Frank and Viola, Babe's ten-year-old sister Kathryn, his older brother Bud and Bud's wife Violet, who was also pregnant, and now Babe and Nora. It was not a happy arrangement.

Nora became the object of cutting remarks and innuendoes from the Gall family, especially Babe's mother. An opinionated, spiteful, sharp-edged woman given to equally sharp words, Viola was an expert in the art of wounding the wounded. Nora was the underdog, the outsider, the naughty little Amish girl deserving of scorn and derision. In one of Viola's caustic attacks she implied that Babe probably wasn't the only boy Nora had been with, and how did they know the baby she was carrying was really his.

Lonely and desperate, Nora turned elsewhere for help and comfort. She began attending the North Main Street Mennonite Church a few blocks down the street. The women there took her under their motherly wings, gave her baby clothes, shared their practical wisdom, and enrolled her baby in the church's Cradle Roll Department. They welcomed the teenage mother and her baby with open arms.

Three days after her sixteenth birthday, Nora gave birth to a baby girl. Two and a half months later, on August 26, 1928, Babe and Nora were married. Quietly, in the home of a local minister named Henry Wysong, the two teenagers said their marriage vows. With the minister's wife as their witness, they pledged to be faithful to each other for as long as they both should live. They kept those vows until Babe's death forty-two years later at age sixty.

I was that baby girl, the firstborn of Babe and Nora's seven children.

∽ 2 ∽

Little Gray House in the Marsh

When I was one and a half, my brother Wilfred joined the Gall family in the crowded apartment on South Main Street. The household now numbered ten: Grandpa and Grandma Gall, Kathryn (now twelve), Bud and Violet and their one-year-old Richard, Babe and Nora, their toddler Shirley (that was me) and baby Wilfred. The togetherness was becoming too much of a good thing.

A long flight of stairs on the outside of the building, next to the alley, led up to Grandpa and Grandma Gall's apartment. Just inside the door at the top of the stairs was a small sitting room with a big wooden rocking chair that I liked to climb into and rock.

One day while sitting in the big rocking chair, I was picking buggers and enjoying the salty taste on my tongue when Grandma Gall walked in.

"Jean!" she said in her sharp accusing voice, "are you eating buggers?" She always called me by my middle name, Jean, which annoyed and upset Mama.

"No," I said, sensing this was something she did not approve of. But I knew she didn't believe me. I didn't believe me either.

In this small room were Grandma Gall's sewing machine and her button basket filled with all kinds of buttons. Big buttons, little buttons, buttons of many colors and shapes and sizes. I liked to sit on the linoleum floor with buttons spread out all around me, sorting, scooting them around and listening to the sounds they made on the linoleum floor. The buttons could become anything I wanted them to be – animals, people, cars, trains, trees, houses.

Soon after Wilfred's birth we left the apartment in Nappanee and moved to a weather-beaten little gray farmhouse on a narrow dirt road east of town. I remember this event because I got to ride with Uncle Harve on the horse-drawn farm wagon that carried our meager household goods. I felt very special perched beside him on the wagon's high wooden seat.

The U.S. Census of April 1930 shows us living in Union Township near Pa and Ma Mitchell. Wilfred's age was listed as 3/12 year (three months), and mine as 1 9/12 years. Thurlo, the head of household, was 20 and Nora was 17. The same census record shows my great-grand-parents, Francis M. Mitchell and Anna E. Mitchell, living nearby. He was 72 and she was 66.

We called the low-lying farmland east of Nappanee "The Marsh." The little gray house sat amid fields of rich black muck dirt, ideal for growing potatoes and mint. In summer the sweet smell of spearmint and peppermint filled the air. At harvest time the mint was cut and hauled to a "mint-distill," which I always thought was a "mintny-still." Here, in big vats, the sweet oils were processed out and sold for medicinal uses or for flavoring candy and chewing gum. The dried leaves and stems became feed for the cattle and horses. I don't remember whether the cows gave mint-flavored milk.

The little gray house had only a kitchen and a living room on the main floor. The living room doubled as Mama and Daddy's bedroom.

One afternoon when I was supposed to be taking a nap in their bed, I began to wonder how close to the edge I could get without falling off. Inch by inch I eased closer to the edge until I reached the tipping point and gravity took over. I fell to the floor with a thump that brought Mama to see what had happened. How does a three-year-old explain that she was performing a scientific experiment?

Wilfred and I slept upstairs in a bedroom with a sloping ceiling. One morning when we came downstairs we discovered a new little baby in a wooden cradle at the foot of the bed. It was Arden, born when I was three and Wilfred was not yet two. By then, Mama was nineteen and Daddy was twenty-one. It was 1931, and the Depression was two years old. Daddy worked as a farmhand and Mama had her hands full caring for three little children and making ends meet.

Outside the back door of the little house in the marsh was a well with cold flowing spring-water. The well pit served as Mama's refrigerator, where she kept milk and eggs and butter cool.

Farther from the house was a two-hole outhouse with its distinctive smells and a Sears and Roebuck catalog. The nearby mint fields acted as a natural air freshener. One day when Mama was sitting on the toilet I stuck my head down the other hole and announced that she had a black beard down there!

In front of the house a drainage ditch ran between the yard and the road, with a plank across it to the mailbox. The ditch emptied into a larger drainage ditch that ran along the edge of the farm. The bridge across the big ditch was called the pontoon bridge, but I never knew why it had that name.

One day when I was playing in the yard I saw a big snake about two feet in front of me, between me and the house. Paralyzed with fear, I stood still and screamed for Mama. She came with Daddy's axe and chopped the snake's head off. It could have been a little garter snake, but I remember it as a huge red snake about six feet long.

A few years ago, Wilfred, Arden, Bill and I revisited the site of the old gray house. The narrow dirt road was now only a farm trail and closed to traffic. We followed it anyway, until we came to the narrow bridge spanning the drainage ditch. The place where the little gray house had stood was overgrown with weeds. Arden explored and found where the well had been. Nothing else showed that a house had once stood there.

My early memories are all that remain of the little gray house in the marsh.

3

Angels on Duty

On a hot August day in 1936 I plodded along the gravel road from our house to the corner a hundred miles away to wait for the big yellow school bus. Unaccustomed to wearing shoes in summer, I could not resist kicking the dirt and stones and watching the little dust clouds rise and fall. My black shoes soon turned to dusty gray.

In one hand I carried a shiny Karo syrup bucket containing my lunch. With the other I clung to the hand of the big girl beside me. She was walking with me to the corner because Mama had my three little brothers and a brand-new baby to take care of. The big girl lived in Chicago and was visiting her grandpa, Ellis Smith, in the big house next door to us. Daddy worked for Ellis Smith on his farm. We had moved twice since the little gray house in the marsh, first to a place on State Road 5 north of Ligonier (where Howard was born), and then to the Smith farm southwest of Ligonier.

Little butterflies of worry and excitement fluttered in my stomach as we waited for the bus. The big girl would not be here to meet me after school, because she was going back to Chicago today. Would I have to walk this long road home all by myself?

The bus came, its folding door opened, and the bus driver greeted me with a smile. I climbed up the three huge steps and found a place to sit on one of the long bench seats. The other children on the bus stared at me, the frightened little red-haired girl with the Karo syrup bucket.

All the way to school I worried about what to do when we got there. How would I know where to go? How would I find my classroom? How would I know what to do? What if I had to go to the bathroom?

The bus driver showed me to my classroom and introduced me to my teacher, who taught first and second grade at the four-room country school named Perry School. Teacher showed me where to put my lunch pail and led me to a desk at the front of the second row.

She rang a little bell and asked everyone to be quiet and listen. She welcomed the first-graders and told us what to expect. She was kind and gentle, but firm. I liked her from the start. School was going to be fun.

All day long, however, I worried about what to do at the end of the day. How would I find the right bus for the ride home? What if I got on the wrong bus? As if she knew my fears, teacher took care of that problem. She walked all of us to where the buses were waiting, and helped each of us find the right bus to take us home.

On the bus I worried again. I was a little nobody. Was the driver going to drop me off at the corner where he'd picked me up in the morning? Would I have to walk the hundred miles from the corner back to my house all by myself? How would I find my way all alone? I worried and worried. Then I had an idea. If the driver knew my family's name, maybe he would know where I lived. I tried to work up enough courage to speak.

Just before we got to The Corner, I found my voice and announced, "My name is Gall." The children on the bus laughed. I blushed with embarrassment. The bus driver smiled at me in the mirror and said, "I know." And he drove right to my house, opened the door and let me out in my own driveway.

Mama was waiting for me with baby sister Carol and my three little brothers. In the kitchen she had cookies and milk waiting for me.

All day long I had worried and worried. All day long I was nervous and afraid about what would happen to me. All day long I was anxious because I didn't know what to expect. And all day long there were people watching out for me, doing their jobs, taking care of a frightened little girl facing a big scary world for the first time. She didn't know the plan, but they did.

One night, not long after that, I woke up and saw someone in a long white gown standing in the hallway outside my bedroom door. I held my breath, afraid to move. The person in white stood watching me for a long time, and then was gone. I had never heard about guardian angels, but I believe I saw mine that night.

All day, all night, all my life, God has had angels on duty, watching out for me when I didn't know it. Some of them were ordinary people doing their jobs, and some were the invisible kind. They have guided and cared for me through every frightening new experience. I don't always know the plan, but he does. What's more, he knows my name, and that's enough.

Shirley in first grade, 1934

⟫ 4 ⟪

Learning About God

Sitting at Mama's feet in the front yard, I learned to sing, "Jesus loves me, this I know, for the Bible tells me so." At her feet I memorized Psalm 86:1, "Bow down thine ear to me, O Lord; hear me, for I am poor and needy."

That may seem like an odd verse to teach a little child, but during those Depression years we were indeed a poor and needy family. I can still hear Mama singing, with a catch in her voice and tears in her eyes, "Does Jesus Care?" She must have wondered.

Her father, Ed Miller, was dying with cancer. He died on September 7, 1934, at age sixty. The following year she lost two more close family members: her brother Eli, age thirty-five, who died of a ruptured appendix on May 16, 1935, and her sister Clara, age nineteen, who died with pneumonia in childbirth on November 22, 1935.

Mama and Daddy, still in their early twenties, already had five children. Two more babies came later, Verna when Mama was twenty-six and Sonja when she was twenty-eight. They worked long and hard, and somehow managed to provide for all of us.

We never lived in one place more than a year or two. Daddy worked as a farmhand for twenty dollars a month and a place to live. They always managed to have a cow to give us milk and butter, and chickens to give us eggs and meat. Mama raised a big garden and made the twenty dollars stretch to the end of the month.

At the outset of their marriage, Ma Mitchell had given Nora sound advice about money management.

"Now Nora," she said, "you tell Babe to give you his earnings and you manage how it's spent." Mama followed that advice.

Before I finished first grade we moved to Edwardsburg, Michigan, to a little gray house on Redfield Road. I finished first grade and started second at Edwardsburg Elementary School. Soon we moved again and lived for a short time with Grandma Miller south of Nappanee. While there I attended a one-room country school with mostly Amish children.

We moved to Wakarusa the last week of December that year, when I was in second grade. Multicolored Christmas lights and a big Christmas tree in the middle of the town square welcomed us to our new hometown. Daddy had been hired to work at the greenhouse on West Waterford Street.

Compassionate people from the Missionary Church (Mennonite Brethren in Christ at that time), one of four churches in town, noticed the new family and took us under their wings. They brought us food and clothing, warm blankets and other household necessities. By their deeds of kindness they showed us God's love. We soon became regulars at Sunday school and church.

One Sunday morning the following August, we all got dressed for church as usual, but instead of going to church in town we went to camp meeting a few miles away. Services at church were canceled to allow everyone to attend camp meeting.

In the children's tabernacle that morning I heard the good news that *God loves me.* He loves me so much that he sent his Son to die for me so that I could have my sins forgiven. I had thought of God as a dreadful and powerful person who lives up in the sky and is always watching what I do, and I'd better be good or he would punish me. That was bad news, because even as a little child I couldn't always be good, no matter how hard I tried. And I did try very hard.

In the children's tabernacle that morning at Prairie Camp Meeting I went forward to confess my sins and receive Jesus as my Savior. I was so happy I couldn't wait to tell Mama. I found her on the path leading to the big tabernacle.

"Mama, guess what," I said. "I invited Jesus into my heart!"

Mama did not acknowledge or react to my announcement of the most important news of my life. That troubled me for years. As an adult I came to understand that she was preoccupied with gathering the five of us, making sure we were clean and toileted and behaving ourselves appropriately. That was a big order.

That morning at Prairie Camp Meeting, the little girl who was a *nobody* became a *somebody* in God's family.

5

Hazardous Environment

The Smith place, where we lived when I was in first grade, presented more than the usual number of hazards for small children. There was a big unfenced yard, an abandoned house behind the house we lived in, the owner's house and yard next door to us, two barns and barnyards, workhorses and farm equipment, and a nearby creek.

And behind our house was an open cesspool, reeking of raw sewage from the upstairs bathroom. (This was one of the few places we ever lived that had an indoor bathroom.) The septic tank had been opened for cleaning and had not been closed up again. It was a headache for Mama and a magnet for four-year-old Wilfred. One day he fell into the six-foot-deep hole and was trapped in sewage up to his waist. Mama was eight months pregnant and frantic at the prospect of her child drowning in the foul mess. I don't know how she managed to get him out. Perhaps she called for Daddy to come and rescue him.

One summer day three-year-old Arden went missing. Gone without a trace. We called for him. No answer. We searched for him everywhere we could think of, inside and outside the house, in our yard and Mr. Smith's yard, under porches, in the old house used as a storage shed behind our house, in the two barns and barnyards, up and down the road and the nearby creek bank. Not a sign of him anywhere. Then, as I made one more circuit around the house, I spotted him near the side door, curled up in a galvanized washtub, fast asleep in the sunshine.

In our search, we had probably passed the spot a dozen times without seeing him. I became the heroine of the day.

The old abandoned house presented many enticements and numerous hazards for little children: broken windows, rickety floors and stairs, and toxic substances for starters. An old wooden box with a hinged lid and a hasp closure was another.

One day a neighbor boy and his mother came to visit. While our mothers chatted in the kitchen, we explored the old house. Wilfred and I and Lyle, the neighbor boy, climbed inside the big wooden box and sat shoulder to shoulder, knees to chins, packed in like three peas in a pod. Suddenly the lid came down and the hasp closed, trapping us inside. We screamed and cried for help and pounded on the walls of the box, but we were too far from the house for our cries to be heard. Something (or someone) told Mama to come looking for us. She rescued us from our dark, cramped prison, and warned us to stay out of the old house.

We promised, but of course it was not the last time we went exploring in the old house.

One day our exploring took us upstairs, where we found a curious little round box on a ledge in the wall. It contained a substance we didn't recognize. We took it to Mama to find out what it was. She went ballistic, and so did Daddy when she showed it to him.

"It's dynamite!" said Daddy. "Where did you find this?"

We led him up the stairs of the old house and showed him where the little box had been stowed. He searched for other hazardous substances—and warned us once again to stay out of that old house. This time we did.

≈ 6 ≈

Friends

On the first day of school after Christmas vacation, Miss Hollopeter stood in front of her second grade class at Wakarusa Elementary School and welcomed her students.

"Boys and girls," she said, "we have a new student in class today. She and her family have just moved to our town. Her name is Shirley."

The shy little red-haired girl blushed and squirmed in her seat as everyone turned to look at her. For the third time in less than a year she was the new girl in class.

"Now, at recess time," Miss Hollopeter continued, "I want some of you girls to introduce yourselves to Shirley and welcome her to our class. She will need some friends to play with."

At recess the shy little girl stood against the wall in the hallway outside the second grade room, wondering whether anyone would be her friend. Three smiling little girls approached.

"Hi," said the first one. "Welcome to our school. We'd like to be your friends. My name is Garna Lee."

"And I'm Joan," said the second one.

"And I'm Faye," said the third.

"Do you want to play with us?" asked Garna.

That was the start of a friendship that lasted throughout their school years until their graduation from high school in 1946. And it didn't stop with graduation. Their friendship has continued for six decades, even though they seldom see each other, and only at class reunions.

The miles have separated the four friends. Faye (Eshelman) Bedward is the only one who still lives in Wakarusa. Joan (Culp) Mayberry lives in New Mexico and Garna Enders in Florida. And the shy little red-haired girl now lives in Wilmore, Kentucky.

Whenever I think about friendship, I think of Garna, Joan and Faye, three little girls who welcomed me, the new girl in their class, and became her true friends. The little girl inside of me is still grateful, and so is the woman I have become.

7

Dreams

At age five or six I had a vivid and terrifying dream of what I can only call hell. I was teetering on a precipice, and below me were flames and ugly, scary creatures. Just before falling into the flames I woke up, relieved to find myself safe at home in my bed.

Throughout my childhood I had dreams of sitting on the toilet and peeing—then I would wake up to find I had wet the bed!

"Shirley! Did you pee to bed again?" Mama would ask with exasperation.

Embarrassed, I would answer "No!" The problem continued into my teens, worsened by the fact that we had no indoor toilet, and a trip to the outhouse in the dark was scary.

During my preteen and early teen years I often dreamed of flying. These dreams were so vivid that I was convinced I really *could* fly. No one believed me, though, and eventually I stopped believing it myself.

My flying dreams took several forms: In one version, I could stand at the top of the stairway and jump all the way to the bottom, floating and gliding to a gentle landing in the living room below, where everyone would be amazed at what I could do. In another version, I could stand in the front yard and jump, like on a trampoline, except that I had never seen a trampoline, and bounce higher and higher until I was above the treetops. In a third version, I could go running down the road, faster and faster, until my feet no longer touched the ground and I was floating through the air, my legs still running to propel me along.

I also dreamed of falling. Falling out of bed, off a roof, out of a tree, or off a wagon. These dreams always woke me up with a violent jerk to find myself safe in bed.

Sometimes I dreamed of encounters with real people and being able to tell them exactly what I wished I could tell them in my waking hours.

And then there were daydreams. Dreams of what I would be and do when I grew up. Dreams of becoming a great writer, a great artist, a great teacher, or a great missionary. I did become a writer, an artist, a teacher and a missionary, but I never became great or famous. At this point in my life, I doubt that I ever will.

I had dreams of meeting a handsome man who would fall madly in love with me and we would be married and live happily ever after. At age forty I met the handsome man who fell madly in love with me. His name was Bill McMillan. We were married and lived together as husband and wife for twenty-eight years, sometimes happily and sometimes not, until depression stole away his joy and eventually his life.

After Bill's death I was puzzled about why I did not see him in my dreams. Then one night I saw him, but only from the back. I recognized his familiar form and distinctive gait as he walked away without looking back. How could he do that, I wondered—just walk away from me, from life, from family, from everything, as if we were nothing.

These days I rarely have a dream that I remember. Is it because dreams are only for the young? Or is my memory bank filled up, with no room left for dreaming?

~ 8 ~

Wit, Wisdom and Work

Mama had a saying for nearly every situation. If someone started to say something and forgot what it was, "It must have been a lie," she said.

When her nose itched, "We must be getting company."

When her ears itched, "Someone must be talking about me."

When someone dropped the dishrag, "Some fool's either coming or going away."

When someone complained about the weather, or about anything else, she said:

"As a rule a man's a fool.
When it's hot he wants it cool.
When it's cool he wants it hot,
Always wanting what is not,
Never content with what he's got."

Mama's rule for good health: "Keep your bowels open and your nose clean."

Before TV and the Weather Channel she had her way of predicting the weather:

"Evening red and morning gray
Sends the traveler on his way.
Evening gray and morning red
Brings down rain upon his head."

25

"In one door and out the other brings bad luck," said Mama, but we knew the only kind of luck she believed in was what people bring on themselves.

No one but salesmen, preachers and Jehovah's Witnesses ever used the front door at our house. Mama didn't allow the Jehovah's Witnesses to get a foot inside. The Watkins salesman and the preacher came in the front door and went out the same way. Everyone else used the back door.

The closest Mama ever came to telling us the facts of life was her little story about Sam, Dan and Sadie.

"What do you want to be when you grow up?" asked their teacher.

Sam stood and said: "My name is Sam. When I grow up to be a man, I'm going to be a farmer if I can, and I think I can."

Sadie was next: "My name is Sadie. When I grow up to be a lady, I'm going to have a baby if I can, and I think I can."

Last of all came Dan: "My name is Dan. When I grow up to be a man, I'm going to help Sadie with her plan if I can, and I think I can."

Although our family was never accused of being cultured, Mama and Daddy maintained strict rules of behavior at the table.

1. Don't talk with your mouth full.
2. Don't chew with your mouth open.
3. Don't smack your lips or make noises when you eat.
4. Eat everything on your plate.
5. No whining, pouting or complaining, or you'll
   get something to complain about.
6. No farting at the table, or you have to go outside and air out.
7. No sassing, or you go to bed without supper.

Personal hygiene rules that are a given today did not apply to us. Since we had no bathroom and no running water, we couldn't bathe or shower every day. Bathing was a once-a-week event on Saturday night, in a galvanized washtub in front of the kitchen stove. The littlest kids got their baths first, then the older ones in order of age. "Don't pee in the bathwater" was the rule here, but you could never be sure your younger siblings hadn't. Being the oldest was definitely not an advantage when it came to Saturday night baths.

Our hair got shampooed once a week, or every other week, using Watkins coconut oil shampoo in a dishpan of water. Mama liked to use rainwater if we had it, because it was "soft." Our well water was so hard we had to be careful not to break our teeth on it, and so mineral-rich it tasted like iron and left thick calcium deposits in the teakettle. After shampooing, we added vinegar to the rinse water to cut the soap scum and make our hair silky and shiny.

Changing underwear every day was not an option, since we seldom had more than one or two pairs at a time. The same went for socks, shoes, shirts, pants and dresses.

To save our school clothes for wearing again the next day, Mama made us change into everyday clothes as soon as we got home from school. And we girls always had to wear an apron to "save our dress" when helping in the kitchen.

One pair of shoes had to do for both school and church. We wore older shoes for everyday, if there was an older pair that we could still get our feet into, and shoes with some wear left in them were passed down to the next in line. It was my job to polish all the "good shoes" on Saturday night. In summer we went barefoot at home from May to September. We often wanted to go barefoot in April, but Mama made us wait until May. "On the first day of May, throw your shoes and socks away" was the rule here.

We ironed clothes with a flatiron on the kitchen table, using old sheets for padding. Mama showed me how to test the iron's heat by touching a finger to my tongue and then to the iron and listening for the sizzle. She taught me to judge the oven's heat by opening the door and putting a hand inside to "feel" how hot it was.

Mama taught me how to clean and fill the kerosene lamps, trim the wicks and wash the lamp chimneys. Before we ever saw a floating-blade vegetable peeler, she showed me how to hold a paring knife just so and peel potatoes nice and thin so as not to waste any of the potato. She taught us how to shell peas and snap beans and husk sweet corn for supper, and how to pit cherries and scald tomatoes and peaches for canning.

In later years Mama sometimes lamented about my having to work so hard when I was growing up.

"Don't worry about that," I told her. "I'm glad you taught me to work hard and make do with whatever there was. I needed to know those things when I was out on my own, and that was especially true in Nigeria."

Still I'm thankful that some of the things Mama taught me are skills I don't need today. She taught me how to scald and pluck a chicken and cut it up for frying. I *hated* the smell of scalding hot chicken feathers! Now I bring a package of skinless, boneless chicken breasts home from the store and leave the backs, necks, wings, legs and giblets for other people to deal with.

≈ 9 ≈

Washday on the Farm

Washday on the farm was an all-day affair that began with getting up early to pump water by hand from the well in the back yard.

It took bucket after bucket to fill the copper boiler heating on the wood-burning stove and the two galvanized washtubs on the rack next to the gasoline-powered Maytag washing machine. When the water in the boiler was heated, it went into the washing machine, and the boiler had to be filled again.

Mama added lye to the water in the boiler, plunged the white clothes into the lye water, and stirred them with her stirring stick made from an old broom handle. With the same stick she transferred the clothes to the washing machine to be agitated in hot soapy water.

Before the Maytag, Mama washed clothes with homemade lye soap on a washboard in a tub of water. The Maytag was a wonderful invention, intended to make washday easier, but getting the engine started could be a problem. Over and over and over, Mama would wind the pulley-rope around the flywheel and yank, like starting a lawnmower. Over and over, the engine would respond with a weak sputter, a single "putt," or nothing at all. Sometimes she yanked and pulled until she had to admit defeat and give up in tears.

White clothes went into the wash water first, followed by lightly soiled colorfast items, then the darker and dirtier pieces, and finally the heavily soiled socks and denim overalls. When a load was finished washing, every item had to be lifted from the water and fed through the hand-operated wringer into the first tub of rinse water, through the wringer into the second rinse, then through the wringer a third time and into a bushel basket lined with oilcloth. The second rinse contained bluing to make white clothes come out sparkling.

Next, the basket of wet clothes had to be carried to the clothesline in the back yard, and the clothes pinned on the line just so, to dry in the fresh air. White clothes flapping on the clothesline were the mark of a good homemaker. "Tattle-tale gray" was a disgrace.

Mama was very particular about how she pinned things on the line with the old-fashioned round clothespins. Each article had to be joined to similar ones on both sides. All the towels must be hung together, pillowcases together, sheets together, and socks, underwear, blouses, shirts, and pants all hung in orderly fashion by categories.

On sunny, breezy days in spring and summer it was a pleasure to see the clean clothes blowing on the line. It was a pleasure to take them down and smell the clean freshness that today's fabric softeners try to mimic, but without success.

Rainy days presented a problem. Our neighbor, Willy Lechlitner, told us that if clothes dried in the rain they would get lousy. I believed him, until I saw his sly "gotcha!" grin.

Winter washdays made summer washdays seem like a breeze. Fingers froze to the pump handle as we pumped water. They froze again as we pinned clothes on the line. Clothes froze stiff as a board and had to be carried into the house to finish drying on a rack by the stove or on lines strung across the room.

Summer or winter, spring or fall, we had to carry all of that wash water and rinse water outside and dump it in the yard. Then supper had to be cooked for a hungry crew. No running out to McDonald's or Papa John's – they hadn't been born yet.

Wash and wear fabric hadn't been invented either, so all those clothes now had to be ironed nice and smooth—but that's another story, another day. The rigors of washday left no time or energy for ironing, hence the old saying, "Wash on Monday, iron on Tuesday, mend on Wednesday...."

After electricity came to the farm, an electric washing machine with a power wringer replaced the gasoline-powered model. The wringer, activated with the push of a button, eased the labor of washday but added a hazard not encountered before. Fingers, hands or long hair could get caught in the wringer, and the rollers would keep right on rolling until someone pushed the stop button.

We heard tales of persons losing an arm in a wringer, or even their hair and scalp. It must have been a very hot summer day when a minimally dressed woman with pendulous breasts got one of them caught in the wringer and couldn't reach the button to stop it. According to reports, it was not a pretty sight.

⤳ 10 ⤳

Pa Mitchell's Model T

The first car I remember was a black Model T Ford with a rumble seat. It belonged to my great-grandfather, known to us as Pa Mitchell. He was Grandma Gall's father. Somewhere in Mama's box of black-and-white photos was a picture of Pa Mitchell's Model T, which is probably the reason I remember it.

Pa Mitchell was tall and thin and wiry, and he wore round glasses with black wire rims. Daddy used to tell us that Pa Mitchell was so limber he could sit on the floor and bend forward until his nose touched the floor, even when he was an old man. Now that I am in my seventies I find that story quite amazing. Unbelievable actually. What I do remember about Pa Mitchell was seeing him stop, grab his chest and bend over in pain. Angina, no doubt.

Pa Mitchell died at seventy-eight, when I was eight years old. As one of his great-grandchildren I was designated to carry flowers and follow his casket out of the little country church in Gravelton, where his funeral was held.

Daddy and Mama also had a Model T after we moved from the marsh to a house north of Ligonier. It may have been the same one that had belonged to Pa Mitchell, but I will never know that for sure, since there is no one alive that I can ask.

I have two memories connected with Daddy's Model T. The first is of Mama trying to drive it out of the farm shed that served as a garage. She had not mastered the art of shifting gears or using the brakes.

Instead of backing out through the door, she drove through the back wall of the shed, and the car stopped with its wheels hanging over the barnyard six feet below.

The second memory of that car is of Daddy and Uncle Toby trying to start it. Two people had to work together to accomplish this, one in front to turn the crank and one inside to adjust the choke and throttle. The Model T was an ornery beast with a mind of its own, and often required multiple attempts to get it going. If it was in a really bad mood, the man at the crank could end up with a broken arm.

I don't know what happened to Daddy's Model T. I don't think he had it for long, because it was not large enough for a family with four little children (five when Carol came along). A Whippet with a back seat replaced the Model T.

≈ 11 ≈

We Were So Poor That...

...We literally didn't have a pot to pee in. When it was too cold to go to the outhouse we used a five-gallon bucket in the "back room."

...We couldn't change into clean clothes every day. Sunday morning we put on clean socks and underwear and wore them the whole week. The dirty ones from the previous week got washed on Monday. As soon as we got home from school we had to change into everyday clothes and save our school clothes to wear the next day.

...Mama often went without underwear at home because hers was either in the wash or she was saving it to wear to church.

...We recycled *everything*, out of necessity, not concern for the environment.

...We wore hand-me-downs until they were rags, and then used the rags for dishrags, dust rags and cleaning rags – after removing buttons, zippers, snap fasteners and hooks-and-eyes for reuse.

...The kitchen table served as our ironing board, and worn-out sheets as ironing pads.

...Old sheets were also ripped up and folded to use as menstrual pads.

...Old socks got darned and worn again until there was nothing left to darn.

...Our shoes got half-soled, re-heeled, re-stitched and passed down to the next younger kid in the family. Daddy and Mama once went without buying groceries for a whole month so they could buy shoes for Wilfred and me. After that month, Daddy said he never wanted to eat potato soup again.

…The "new" little red wagon that appeared on Christmas morning was our old rusty one sanded and repainted.

…The only doll I remember having was a hand-me-down from a neighbor girl. The doll lost her head, arms and legs when she was left outside in the rain overnight.

…We made ice cream by mixing cream, sugar and vanilla with fresh clean snow.

…Mama made dresses from printed flour sacks, and dishtowels from the plain ones.

…We carried our lunch to school in a Karo syrup bucket.

…Daddy picked up coal by the railroad tracks and carried it home to heat our house.

…On Saturdays he drove to Huffman's Bakery in Nappanee where he could buy a big feed sack of day-old bread for a quarter.

…Snow blew in through the cracks in our bedroom windows and made little drifts on the windowsills.

…Daddy sprayed water on the outside of the house and let it freeze over to keep the wind from blowing through the cracks.

…When Wilfred, Arden and I heard Daddy and Mama discussing what to do about the yard because they couldn't afford a lawn mower, we told them they didn't need to buy one. We would "mow" the grass with our hands, down on our knees. We actually tried this, but quickly learned it wouldn't work.

…I felt really rich when I found a dime in the floor register above the furnace, and Mama said I could keep it. It was the first money I'd ever had to call my own.

…We saved chewing gum to be reused, and sometimes traded gum wads with each other. When we didn't have gum we chewed paraffin, and once we tried chewing street tar softened by the summer sun. Once was enough.

…In the fifth grade I withheld my name from the Christmas drawing because I felt that twenty-five cents was more than my parents could afford to give me to buy a gift for the exchange. On the day of the class Christmas party, I was surprised to hear my name called and to see a gift for me, due to the kindness of a little girl named Laurabelle Eby, who thought I should not go home without a gift.

…The nicest clothes I ever had were hand-me-downs from girls in more well to do families.

Gall family, 1941. Clockwise from top: Daddy, Mama (holding Sonja), Howard, Carol, Verna, Arden, Wilfred, Shirley

➡ 12 ⬅

The Secret

"School's out! School's out! Teacher let the monkeys out!" It was still April, but in Wakarusa, school was out for the summer.

We were finished with fourth grade and our stern, no-nonsense teacher, Miss Searer. I would soon be ten years old and ready for fifth grade with Mr. Conrad. Until then, four months of summer stretched ahead.

First there would be two weeks of vacation Bible school, then three months of summer fun, or three months of summer work, depending on who you were. My summer would be mostly filled with work. Mama needed my help with our big vegetable garden, and with cleaning, laundry, ironing, cooking, baking, canning, and looking after my four younger siblings ranging from eight to not quite four years old.

One hot day in the middle of August, Mama took me aside for a talk, a most unusual occurrence. Mama never had time to just talk.

"There's something I need to tell you," she said. She seemed uneasy, and I wondered what was up. Was I in trouble? What had I done?

"I'm going to tell you a secret," she announced. "But I want you to promise you won't tell anybody."

"I promise," I said, feeling important.

"I'm going to tell you where babies come from," she said. It was a subject I hadn't thought too much about since the time the doctor brought my sister Carol in his black bag in the middle of the night when I was six. That was four years ago.

Mama twisted the corner of her apron, and then laid her hands on her stomach.

"Have you noticed that my belly is getting bigger?" she asked. I hadn't really noticed, but now that she mentioned it, I could see that it was. What on earth did that have to do with the subject of babies?

"My belly is getting big because it has a baby growing inside. We're going to have a baby in September."

She's got to be kidding, I thought. *How could a baby get inside Mama's belly? How could it live in there? How would it get out?*

But I didn't ask. I was too stunned and too shy to ask. I didn't say a word. I just waited for Mama to tell me more, but she didn't. I think she was too shy and embarrassed to tell me more.

"Now I want you to go pick green beans for supper," she said. "Here's a pan. Pick enough to fill it."

Bursting with importance at the astounding new information, I went to the garden to pick beans. But beans were not on my mind as I bent over the rows. An information explosion had just taken place in my brain, and I couldn't wait to tell Wilfred what I knew. Would he ever be surprised!

On the porch swing that evening I whispered to Wilfred, "You'll never guess what Mama told me today."

"What?" he asked.

"If I tell you, you've got to promise not to tell anybody. Promise?"

"Promise," he said.

"Cross your heart?"

"Cross my heart."

"Cross your heart and hope to die?"

"Cross my heart and hope to die, Devil catch me if I lie."

I leaned closer and whispered in his ear. "Mama told me where babies come from, and you'd never guess in a million years! They come from their mama's belly!"

"Huh! I knew that," he said. "Everybody knows that. I'm surprised you didn't."

So much for feeling important.

⟹ 13 ⟸

Longings

Growing up during the Depression years, I longed for many things that I knew I could never have. I longed for beautiful clothes (enough to wear a different dress to school every day), naturally curly hair, a room of my own with pretty curtains at the windows, an indoor bathroom with hot and cold running water—and privacy. I longed for time to read and daydream and do whatever I wanted.

And I longed to have a violin. I used to leaf through the Sears and Roebuck "wish-book" in the outhouse and wish for many things, but I dreamed of having a violin. The Sears catalog featured violins for only twenty-five dollars, plus shipping and handling, but the price might as well have been twenty-five hundred, or twenty-five thousand. In our family there was rarely twenty-five cents to spare, and never twenty-five dollars.

I had never seen or heard anyone play a violin, and I had never seen or heard an orchestra. But the violin in the catalog was so beautiful, with its sensuous curvy lines and shiny finish. I just knew it would sound beautiful too, if I could ever get my hands on one and learn to play it. I never did. The closest I came to it was years later when I learned to play a saw using a violin bow.

Another thing I longed for was a bicycle. One summer at our Miller Reunion, cousin Ada showed up with a shiny new blue bicycle, and she let the rest of us take turns riding it. I had never been on a bicycle before, but that afternoon I kept trying and trying until I learned how to ride. Oh joy! I wanted to ride and ride and never stop, but I had to take turns with all the other cousins. Since then I have often marveled at Ada's generosity in allowing us to ride her brand-new bicycle, and I've wondered how many scratches and dings it had at the end of that day.

After that I used to watch other kids riding their bikes and think, "Before I ever get a bike I'll be too old to ride one." I thought no one older than sixteen rode a bicycle.

When I finally got a bicycle it was not really mine. It was an old rusty boys' bike, and it was for all of us to share. Our bike had balloon tires and a coaster brake and only one gear, but that was fine with us. We had never seen or heard of a three-speed or ten-speed bike with hand brakes and skinny tires.

With sandpaper and paint we set about refurbishing our bicycle to make it look "new."

We sanded away the rust and smoothed the old chipped finish, and we painted our bike "sea-foam green" with paint from the Montgomery Ward catalog. We painted the wheels and spokes with shiny aluminum paint. Our bike was beautiful to us, and it served us well for years.

I used to ride that bike five miles to Wakarusa and five miles back to attend midweek prayer meeting and youth group activities at church. When I was old enough to get a job I rode that bike three miles each way to catch a ride to Elkhart where I worked at Kresge's five-and-ten. I was sixteen and still riding a bike! In fact, I am now in my seventies and I still ride a bike, but mostly it's my stationary bike in the bedroom. I wonder if I'll be able to ride when I'm a hundred.

14

Medicine Cabinet in the Kitchen

"Mama! Mama! A big bumble bee stung me!" I ran into the kitchen screaming and crying. I'd been playing in the big grassy yard dotted with golden dandelions and sweet white clover flowers.

Mama wiped her hands on her apron and reached for the baking soda. She knew just what to do. First, remove the stinger, then apply a paste made of baking soda and water.

This and other home remedies from my childhood are still my standbys today. They are found in the pantry or kitchen cabinet instead of the bathroom medicine cabinet. They are cheaper and often more effective than remedies from the pharmacy.

Baking soda is a tried and true emollient for bee stings, mosquito bites and minor burns. A baking soda soak will soothe and soften aching feet, and a baking soda bath will calm an allover itch.

It's also a good dentifrice. We brushed our teeth with baking soda because we couldn't afford toothpaste. Today, dentists recommend brushing with soda. Toothpaste manufacturers add it to their products and charge a high price for it, but a fifty-cent box of baking soda from the pantry shelf will outperform and outlast a three-dollar tube of toothpaste.

The uses for baking soda are almost endless. It works as a non-abrasive cleaner for countertops, sinks, showers and bathtubs, as a refrigerator deodorizer, and as a laundry additive. A liberal sprinkling of soda on carpets before vacuuming eliminates pet odors.

Ordinary table salt is another useful remedy. No store-bought mouthwash can beat the price or the effectiveness of gargling with warm salt water at the onset of a sore throat. It takes only a teaspoon of salt in half a glass of warm water, and it can be repeated as often as necessary. No need to worry about the cost—a sixty-nine-cent box of table salt will provide about a hundred gargles

One of my favorite sore-throat remedies is apple cider vinegar and clover honey in steaming hot water. This sweet-and-sour drink is delicious at breakfast, lunch, dinner and bedtime, and any time in between. It may not stop the cold, but the vinegar helps to clear the throat and the honey soothes it. White or distilled vinegar will do the trick too, but apple cider vinegar tastes better.

Some folks prefer lemon and honey rather than vinegar and honey. This is fine if you have fresh lemons on hand for squeezing, or if you can make a trip to the grocery store. Apple cider vinegar is less trouble, and in my opinion it's just as tasty as lemon juice.

A steaming cup of strong peppermint tea is a good remedy for clogged sinuses. Fresh peppermint from the garden or dried peppermint leaves from the pantry work equally well. Be sure to use boiling hot water, and have a box of tissues close by. The peppermint vapors and steam will make your eyes water and your nose run.

After contact with poison ivy, wash the exposed area with Fels-Naphtha soap to remove the poisonous "urushiol" that causes the itching, oozing rash of poison ivy, poison oak and poison sumac. Remove and wash clothing too, to prevent transfer of urushiol from clothing to skin. If the dog got into the ivy, he or she will need a bath too, and any tools used near the poison ivy should be thoroughly washed.

My brothers declared that you could immunize yourself to poison ivy by eating the leaves, but I think they made that up. I never tried it. I didn't want poison ivy attacking my insides.

Mama said warm, soapy water is a good healer. We could never use a cut or sore as an excuse to get out of washing dishes. "Soapy water is good for it," she said. "It will help it to heal."

As much as I didn't want to believe that, I think she was right. So guess what—I said the same thing to my son and my granddaughters.

⇒ 15 ⇐

Names and Nicknames

Mama hated nicknames. She wanted each of her children to be called by the name she and Daddy gave us at birth. I got stuck with a nickname anyway: "Pooey Bean." That was what Uncle Toby and my brothers liked to call me. Where did it come from? From my own mouth! When I was learning to talk, "Pooey Bean" was the nearest I could come to saying "Shirley Jean."

My Grandma Gall wanted me to be named Jean Ellen, but Mama had already decided my name would be Shirley. She compromised by naming me Shirley Jean, but Grandma Gall insisted on calling me Jean until the day she died, and so did all of our Gall relatives. When we were with the Galls I was Jean. Everywhere else I was Shirley—most of the time.

Sometimes I was called Red or Pinky or Carrot Top because of my flaming red hair. To some I was Gall Bladder or Gall Stone, for obvious reasons.

Daddy used to say, "Bitter as Gall, sweet after all."

On the farm we had a series of German shepherd dogs named Thunder. They were always outdoor dogs. One day as we were saying grace at the dinner table, Thunder began barking at something in the back yard, right in the middle of our prayer. Upset at this irreverence, four-year-old Sonja ordered through folded hands, "Thunder! Be quiet!"

For a while Carol had a pet chicken named Ethel. Her chicken had been rescued from a barrel of unhatched eggs that Daddy brought home from Weaver's Hatchery to feed the pigs. Due to her rough start in life, Carol's chicken walked with a limp that reminded us of a dear lady at church named Ethel.

One September Mama had bushels and bushels of peaches that needed to be canned *right now*. Mama was pregnant with Sonja, and desperately needed someone to stay home from school and help can the peaches before they spoiled. I was the logical one, since I was the oldest and could have been the most help to her. But I wanted to achieve a perfect attendance record. Why should I have to be the one to stay home? I pleaded and cajoled until Mama gave in.

"Okay," she said, "go on and get your perfect attendance, but someone will have to stay home and help." Daddy reinforced it, and somehow Arden became the chosen one. When he went back to school, word got around that he'd stayed home to help can peaches. His friends began calling him Peaches, and it stuck with him for the rest of his school years in Wakarusa.

I don't remember whether I got that perfect attendance certificate, or what happened to it if I did.

Everyone seemed to have trouble pronouncing and spelling Wilfred. It usually came out as Wilford or Winfred, or some other adulterated form. Eventually he adopted the name Willy, and that's the name everyone called him until the day of his death, but not Mama. To her he was always Wilfred.

"That's the name I gave him, and that's still his name," she said.

Daddy's name was Thurlo Charles Wilfred Gall, a fine name and one to be proud of. But in the Gall family he was always Babe. He had been the baby of the family for seven years, until his sister Kathryn was born. All his life he was Babe or Uncle Babe to all of our Gall relatives.

Having two middle names was a bother, so he dropped the two middle names and went by Thurlo Gall. When he went to work as a railroad brakeman on the New York Central, his name was posted on the callboard as "T. Gall." He never told anyone what the T stood for, so his coworkers called him Tim. That was his name for all the years he worked on the railroad.

At home, Daddy was always Daddy, until the boys approached their teens and started calling him "Pop." It sounded less childish "Pop" caught on. I called him Pop too, and eventually he was Pop to all seven of us. But now I think of him as Daddy.

Mama was always Mama. In my teens and twenties I felt uncomfortable calling her Mama in front of my friends, but Mother didn't seem to fit, and Mom didn't feel right. To my friends I referred to her as "my mother" or "my mom," but she was Mama, and still is.

Bill was always Bill to me, never William. As a child he was called Billy, but as an adult he tolerated that only from his mother. My term of endearment for him was "Dear." It seemed to fit him just right. It wasn't syrupy or gushy, but expressed my feelings for him. He was a dear.

Jimmy's birth name was James Edward Gall, but he was Jimmy to everyone. At his adoption we kept his full birth name and added McMillan: James Edward Gall McMillan. As he grew and changed, he experimented with different names, and we tried to accommodate by using whatever was his preferred name at the time: Jimmy to James, then Jamey, then Jim, and back to Jimmy. His professional name as a Southern Gospel singer and songwriter is Jimmy McMillan. It fits him well, and it sounds very Southern.

≈ 16 ≈

Crushes

My first crush was a boy named Eddie in first grade. He liked me too. We played together at recess, and one day we kissed. Our romance ended in the spring when we moved to Edwardsburg, Michigan.

During grade school, junior high and high school I had many crushes: boys at school, boys at camp meeting, boys my age, older boys, boys on my school bus, my school bus driver, youth leaders and teachers. In seventh grade I had a crush on my homeroom teacher. He was kind and gentle and soft-spoken and he wore soft-soled shoes that hardly made any noise when he walked, and I thought he was the nicest man I had ever met. I got goose bumps whenever he stood near my desk, and I fantasized that he liked me too.

In junior high a new boy joined our class. He was tall and skinny and walked with a sort of loping gait, and his nose had a bump in the middle where it had been broken, and he was smart – very smart. His desk was just behind mine in homeroom, and I thought he was wonderful, even when he poked and annoyed me. Maybe especially when he poked and annoyed me.

We lived in the middle of a square-mile section, on a narrow dirt road that ended at our house. No one ever used that road unless they were lost or coming to see us. I used to dream about this boy coming down that narrow dirt road to our house to see me, but he never did.

He was so smart that he finished high school early, and while the rest of us were seniors he was already a college freshman. He became a geologist and went on one of the early research expeditions to Antarctica. I went to Bethel College in Mishawaka and then to Nigeria as a missionary.

When I came home on furlough, he dropped by our house on Osborne Road for a visit. He wanted to hear all about my exciting adventures in Africa, but I had nothing exciting or impressive to tell him. I had not seen a single large animal such as elephant or tiger or lion. I had seen lots of lizards inside and outside my house, a viper in my bathroom, a pet monkey that ate my sweet-corn crop, a wild pig or two, a gazelle, some baboons, and a pet parrot that did an exact imitation of my laugh.

The next time I saw my old friend was in Southern California, after I had moved to Los Angeles and married. His mother, who was Mama's good friend, now lived in Southern California too. When Mama came to visit us at Christmas time, we drove to Orange County to visit her friend, and there he was.

He was still tall and skinny and walked with a loping gait and had a funny nose with a bump in the middle where it had been broken, but I no longer had a crush on him.

I was happy to be married to Bill McMillan, the love of my life.

≈ 17 ≈

Family Reunions

Family reunions were a part of every summer when we were growing up.

The Miller Reunion came near the end of June, when we celebrated Grandma Miller's birthday and got together with dozens of cousins, some Amish and some "English" like us. Cars mingled with horses and buggies in the big yard between the house and barn.

The men congregated near the house in the shade of a spreading maple tree to swap tales and discuss the events and issues of the day. In the house the women caught up on family news and set out huge amounts of food on the long serving table.

Young children played under the watchful eyes of their mothers. Older children rode bikes or swung in the haymow or played softball. Teenagers clustered to talk, boys in one group and girls in another.

When all family members had arrived, the call was given to come and eat. As the eldest male Amish relative gave the gesture to pray, all heads bowed for the silent prayer and waited for the clearing of the throat or the scraping of feet that signaled the amen.

We never had to worry about running out of food—there was always more than enough. Our only concern was whether there would be a piece of our favorite pie when we got to the dessert section.

The Gall Reunion, which came in August, was called the Smith Reunion, because Ma Mitchell's family name was Smith. Sometimes it was at Pa and Ma Mitchell's house, sometimes at Aunt Kathryn's or

Aunt Sis's (Edith), or at another relative's home, and once it was at the home of a real Smith who lived on U.S. 12 near Edwardsburg.

One summer the Gall (Smith) Reunion was held at a park beside a lake, but we weren't sure which side of the lake. Hot and sweaty and squished together in a car crammed with seven kids and two adults, we drove round and round trying to find the reunion.

We had nearly given up when someone said, "Why don't we just look for a bunch of redheads. That's bound to be the Galls." The plan worked. We stopped when we saw a gathering of people where about fifty percent were redheads. Mama brought out her specialties to add to the big family feast, and soon everyone was digging in.

One August there was not room enough in the car's trunk for all the food Mama had prepared, so she stashed a custard pie under the front passenger seat. Five-year-old Carol was riding in front with Daddy and Mama, because she always got carsick if she rode in the back seat. The rest of us hated that.

Hot and fidgety, Carol twisted and squirmed until she accidentally put a foot in the pie. Mama was understandably upset. Famous for her custard pies, she was determined the pie would not be a total loss. We stopped at a roadside table on State Road 19 to clean Carol's shoe and salvage as much of the pie as possible. At the reunion Mama set the pie on the serving table with strict instructions to us not to tell anyone what had happened. By meal's end the pie was all gone.

The summer I turned nine, the Gall/Smith Reunion was held at Aunt Sis's house in Gravelton. In mid-afternoon we left the reunion and drove to Stump's Pond on a farm northeast of Nappanee. Our pastor, H. M. Metzger, and lots of people from our church in Wakarusa were there for a baptism service. They sang "Shall We Gather at the River" and other songs after the pastor dipped people under the water and raised them up again. I wasn't quite sure what baptism meant, but I knew it was something very special because people were crying when I came up out of the water.

Among the Galls the way of dealing with differences was not to speak to someone. It seemed that one part of the family was always "on the outs" with another, for offenses known or unknown. If Grandma Gall was not speaking to them, we were not supposed to speak to them. If someone wasn't speaking to us, no one else was supposed to speak to us.

The Smith Reunion died for many years. It revived in the 1990s as the Gall Reunion, with descendants of Frank and Viola Gall meeting at a community building in Syracuse. After a few years it morphed into a gathering of Thurlo and Nora's children and their offspring, and after Mama's death I became the "family matriarch."

For several years, Carol, Verna and I planned the annual event, a family campout at Phil and Verna's Living Waters Campground and Retreat Center near Cassopolis. It took place in September, after their busy camping season ended. Verna and Phil provided campsites, cabins and lodge with kitchen free of charge. The family began gathering on Friday, or even Thursday, for a weekend of food and fun, campfires, crafts, canoeing, games, visiting, a talent show, family auction, family chapel service, and some good-natured practical jokes.

After Phil and Verna sold Living Waters, the reunion morphed again. The planning passed to a younger generation, and the gathering became a weekend campout at the Middlebury KOA. A big potluck meal and family auction on Sunday draw family members who don't wish to camp out for the weekend.

Grandpa and Grandma Gall (Frank and Viola)

≈ 18 ≈

Traditions

Traditions—who needs them? I do, and I think we all do.
Traditions are the ways of doing things that connect us to our family of origin, to our past, and ultimately to our roots. Tradition influences when we put up a Christmas tree, when and how we open gifts, whose house we go to for holiday dinners. Traditions can bind families together and can also divide.

Traditions can be sacred or silly, weighty with significance or so ridiculous that no one knows how or why they got started. Ours were mostly silly.

Our family had a birthday tradition of putting the birthday person under the table and administering a spanking with swats equal to the number of that person's years—plus one to grow on, one to get married on, and one for anything else we could think of. None of us ever thought to ask why we did this. It was a Gall family tradition.

If we went to visit a relative or friend and found them not home, it was our tradition to leave some "sign" that we'd been there. Since few people had a telephone, no one had yet made a rule about phoning ahead if you intend to come over. On a Sunday afternoon Mama and Daddy would pile all of us kids in the car and announce that we were going to take a drive to see Grandma and Grandpa, or Uncle and Aunt So-and-so. If we found no one home, we would look for something to put out of place or upside down as our calling card. It might be lawn chairs or a table, a broom or rake, a wagon or wheelbarrow, a trashcan—

anything that would attract notice. Then we had fun thinking about them coming home and trying to figure out who had been there while they were away.

In those days it didn't take a whole lot to amuse and entertain us.

This calling card tradition was one we practiced only with the Gall family, not with our Miller (Amish) relatives. With the Miller relatives we would leave a note to let them know we'd been there. Or if they had left a note saying they were at another relative's house, we would go there to find them.

About once a year we visited the Weldy (or Welty) Cemetery west of Nappanee, where our Amish relatives were buried. Mama would always cry over the graves of Grandpa Miller, Aunt Clara and her baby, Uncle Eli, and later Uncle Sam and Grandma Miller. She would pull weeds and clip the grass around the plain headstones, which were all the same size, with plain lettering that showed only the deceased person's name, date of birth and date of death. We never planted or laid flowers at the graves, because Amish tradition forbids it.

After Grandma Miller was widowed for the second time, she used to come to our house once or twice a year and stay for a week or two. We looked forward to those visits. She always showed up with a bag of hard candies or mints for us in her battered cardboard suitcase. She would sit in a rocking chair by the window and mend our clothes and socks by hand, and while she mended she would sing. She sang hymns from her German hymnbook and songs we knew from our church hymnal. She told us stories about our mother when she was a little girl.

At bedtime, Grandma went upstairs with us girls to sleep in our room. It was a special privilege to share our bedroom with Grandma. We liked watching her remove her prayer cap and hairpins and let down her long white braids. We liked watching her unpin her long dark dress and cape, and we liked seeing what she wore underneath all that. (She wore a white cotton slip that was like an under-dress, with a full skirt and a bodice fastened with hooks and eyes.) We liked listening to Grandma's *hm-pa, hm-pa* breathing while she slept.

Grandma Miller

Our family all sat down for meals together at the big table in the kitchen. We gave thanks for our food with the table grace,

"God is great, God is good,
And we thank him for our food.
By his hand we all are fed.
Give us, Lord, our daily bread. Amen."

We might say it in unison, or a younger child might be asked to say it.

The kitchen was the center of activity and hospitality. It was a place for visiting, talking, playing games, doing homework, and entertaining guests, but we didn't call it entertaining. We didn't call it hospitality either, but that's what it was. When company came, expected or unexpected, Mama would brew a pot of coffee and set out pie, cake, cookies or other goodies. If they showed up near mealtime, she would ask them to stay for supper. Meals at our house were never fancy, but the food was always hearty and delicious.

The tradition of hospitality has stuck with me for a lifetime. I keep a well-stocked pantry so that I can put a meal together on short notice without going to the grocery store. I don't often have pies and cookies on hand, but there is usually fresh fruit, yogurt and ice cream in the refrigerator. I may have to scramble to clear my table and make space for a tablecloth, place settings and food, but guests are always welcome. In that way I am more like Mama than I ever thought.

Hospitality is a tradition that is sure to bless the recipients, and can bring some wonderful surprises. Maybe even an angel or two, or the Lord himself. "Don't forget to show hospitality to strangers, for some who have done this have entertained angels without realizing it" (Hebrews 13:2). "I tell you the truth, when you did it to one of the least of these my brothers and sisters, you were doing it to me" (Matthew 25:40).

Hospitality is one tradition that I want to keep—and pass on.

Clockwise from top: Daddy, Shirley, Arden, Verna,
Mama holding Sonja, Carol, Howard, Wilfred.

⇒ 19 ⇐

Mama

Mama was pretty and petite, with long, shiny dark hair that she wore in a bun at the back of her neck—until her middle years, when it became okay to have her hair cut short and permed in curls that framed her face.

At home Mama wore a cotton print housedress with an apron to keep her dress clean. If company showed up unexpectedly, she could remove the apron with one quick sweep of her arm and answer the door wearing a clean dress. In those days, before everyone had telephones, company was never expected but always welcome.

Mama's apron was useful for other things as well: wiping wet hands or runny noses, drying tears, gathering eggs from the henhouse or vegetables from the garden, carrying jar lids from the basement to the kitchen for canning summer's bounty.

Every summer Mama canned hundreds of quarts of summer's bounty for winter consumption: peaches, plums, cherries, applesauce, green beans, peas, corn, tomatoes, beets, pickles and relishes, jams and jellies. She filled a ten-gallon crock with sauerkraut and another with dill pickles.

Mama was famous for her homemade bread, pies, cookies, biscuits, shortcake and other baked goodies. I loved the simple but yummy, vanilla-flavored yellow cake that she called "cottage pudding." She often whipped up one of these cakes before breakfast and had it baked and cooled in time to pack squares of it in our school lunches. Sometimes she made a buttery lemon-flavored sauce to pour over it for a delicious finale to supper.

Custard pie was Mama's specialty. No one could make custard pie the way Mama did. For family reunions or potlucks she nearly always made custard pie. Other things too, of course—in fact, several other things, because with our family of seven kids and two adults she wanted to be sure she brought enough food so that no one could accuse her of freeloading.

Daddy loved Mama's pies. "I only like two kinds of pie," he used to say, "single crust and double crust. The only kind I don't like is jam pie, with the top crust jammed against the bottom." Mama never made jam pie.

All of us loved Mama's pies, no matter what kind they were. Especially Howard. One day Mama set a freshly baked pumpkin pie on the table and invited Howard to sample it. He quickly finished off a generous slice and helped himself to another, with the comment, "Mm-mm, that tastes like more!" He devoured the second slice and reached for a third.

Watching in disbelief as the pie disappeared, Carol spoke up. "Mama! Do you see what Howard's doing?"

"Yes," said Mama, unperturbed.

"But do you *see* what he's *doing!*" Carol repeated with indignation.

"Yes," said Mama as she stirred a pot of noodles on the stove.

"It's his pie," she said after a pause.

What Howard knew, and Carol didn't know, was that Mama had baked a *whole pie* for each family member.

"There's one for you too," said Mama, as she and Howard burst into laughter.

Here is Mama's recipe for making a perfect custard pie. She didn't have it written down. I coaxed the directions from her and wrote them myself. These directions may differ slightly from Carol's version. She is the current pie-baking champion in the family.

Mama's Custard Pie

Ingredients for one 9-inch pie:
2 eggs, room temperature
¾ cup sugar
2 tablespoons flour
2 ½ cups milk, room temperature or slightly warmed
Pinch of salt
½ tsp Watkins double-strength vanilla
Cinnamon
Unbaked pie shell

Directions: Take the eggs out of the refrigerator and leave them on the counter overnight to bring them to room temperature. Warm the milk slightly in a saucepan on top of stove (or in a glass container in microwave). Line a glass or enamel pie pan with pie dough; trim and crimp the edges. Beat eggs until frothy. Mix sugar and flour together; add gradually to eggs, and continue beating. Add milk and vanilla and beat again. Pour into prepared pie shell and sprinkle generously with cinnamon. (Never use nutmeg!) Bake at 450 degrees for 10 minutes; reduce heat to 325 and bake about a half hour, until custard is "jiggly." Test for doneness by inserting a knife in the center. If it comes out clean, custard is done.

20

Survival Skills

Survival skills that children learn at Boy Scout or Girl Scout camp were part of everyday life when I was growing up. To cook our food and warm the house we had to know how to build a fire and keep it going. Water for drinking, cooking and washing came from a well with a pump we operated by hand. Sometimes, to get the water flowing we had to prime the pump with a small amount of water kept near the pump for that purpose.

We grew our own food in a big garden and an even bigger "truck patch." We hoed and weeded and tilled. We pulled radishes and onions and carrots, picked peas and beans, tomatoes, strawberries and cucumbers. We husked sweet corn and dug potatoes and sweet potatoes. We helped Mama can hundreds of quarts of fruits and vegetables for winter.

In spring we dug dandelion greens for the table, long before any garden vegetables were ready to eat. With Mama's sweet-and-sour bacon dressing poured hot over the wilted greens and boiled eggs, the greens were delicious.

In summer we went to the woods to pick wild blackberries, rasp-berries and huckleberries. In winter we helped Willy Lechlitner, our neighbor and landlord, gather sap from the maple trees in the woods and cook it into delicious maple syrup. Later, a taffy-pulling party at the Lechlitners' house gave us sweet fun and warmth on a cold winter night.

We had no electricity and no electric lights or appliances: no refrigerator, no toaster, blender, electric mixer or food processor. And of course no television, because this was the pre-television era. We did have a battery-powered radio encased in an oak-veneer cabinet.

At the Lechlitner place the windmill pumped water into an elevated tank by the stairway to give us running water in the kitchen. Most places we pumped and carried it by hand. We heated it on the wood-burning cook stove and washed dishes in a dishpan on the kitchen table. Afterward we emptied the water into the slop bucket or tossed it out the back door. Garbage went into a slop bucket to be carried to the barn and fed to the pigs.

On school days I helped pack the lunches for school. Store-bought bread came wrapped in waxed paper, which we carefully saved for wrapping school-lunch sandwiches. Then we folded and saved the sandwich wrappers to be used again.

On Saturday I helped to trim and fill all the kerosene lamps and wash the lamp chimneys.

On Saturday night we took baths in a washtub in front of the kitchen stove. Summer and winter we used the two-seater outhouse. In summer it was a reading room as we lingered over the Sears and Roebuck or Montgomery Ward catalog, wishing for things we knew we could never have. In the cold of winter we didn't linger, but finished our business as soon as possible and ran back to the house to get warm.

When I went to Nigeria in my mid-twenties, I already knew how to get along without modern conveniences. It was no big deal. I was glad I had learned how to survive and make do. All those things I learned as a child have come in handy throughout my adult life.

⟿ 21 ⟾

Immunizations

Children can't be enrolled in school these days without a certificate showing they've been immunized against most of the common childhood diseases. In my childhood we got immunized by getting the disease.

In first grade I "brought home" from school both the measles and whooping cough and "gave" them to my three brothers. While caring for us, Mama came down with the measles too, and was sicker than all the rest of us together. She was confined to bed in the darkened living room to prevent her from going blind. She had measles splotches outside and inside her body cavities.

While Mama was sick, an Amish "hired girl" came and took care of Mama and us, and did all the cooking and cleaning. Her name was Lizzie Glick. Years later Lizzie became our beloved Aunt Lizzie when Uncle Harve married her after the death of his first wife, Mattie. Uncle Harve and Aunt Lizzie were married for almost 34 years, until her death from thyroid cancer in 2003 at age 88.

Aunt Lizzie was born with only one hand. Her left arm was a stump that ended at the elbow, but Aunt Lizzie was never "handicapped." Her parents immunized her against feeling handicapped by treating her the same as all their other children. She could hold a potato with her stubby arm and peel it as well as any two-handed person. She could cook and clean, wash and iron clothes, do dishes, can fruits and vegetables—you name it, she could do it, and do it well.

When we children caught whooping cough, we whooped and coughed and wheezed for months. Our cousins caught it too, and joined us in whooping and coughing and wheezing. When we drove past their house on US 6 on the way to Nappanee, Daddy would open the car window, lean out and whoop as loud as he could, and we would all laugh. We thought it was exceedingly funny.

When I was in sixth grade and chickenpox was "going around," my siblings got it but it missed me. Mama surmised that I was immune because as a toddler I'd had vareloid, a mild form of smallpox resulting from a vaccination.

Later still, everyone but me got the mumps. The explanation for that was that Mama had the mumps when I was six weeks old and I was immunized through her breast milk.

Polio was a much-feared disease during my youth. In summer the public swimming pools and beaches were closed during the "dog days" of August, in an effort to curb the epidemic. Still this paralyzing disease affected many families in our part of northern Indiana. Children and young people were the most susceptible, but adults also came down with it. Some polio patients had to be confined in an iron lung that did their breathing for them. In the newspaper I saw a picture of such a patient, and I thought it looked something like being in a huge hollow sausage with only the patient's face and head showing. I wondered if it might be better to die than to spend a lifetime in an iron lung.

Polio took lives, disrupted families and left people paralyzed or weakened for life, often with a shriveled and useless arm or leg. When my friend Nora's younger sister was stricken by polio, her mother and sister moved to Dallas to get the best available treatment. In spite of that, Virginia was confined to a wheelchair for much of her life.

When Dr. Jonas Salk developed the first successful polio vaccine, he became a national hero. His vaccine, and succeeding generations of vaccines, changed the face of polio. The dreaded annual epidemic that crippled and killed its victims became a memory from the distant past. Few children and young people today have ever known anyone with polio.

Because of mandatory immunizations, most children in the U.S. will never experience measles, mumps, whooping cough, chicken pox, or any of the other communicable childhood diseases.

What we need now is a universal flu vaccine that will update itself and be effective year after year as the flu virus mutates in its attempt to wipe out the human race.

⁓ 22 ⁓

Halloween Parade

The Halloween parade was a big community event in Wakarusa, with cash prizes for the best costumes. The street was closed to traffic for a block in each direction from the town square. The high school band performed on a wooden bandstand on the corner in front of the Exchange State Bank. Walter Meyers had his popcorn wagon on the opposite corner. There were doughnuts and apple cider and bobbing for apples.

The parade formed at the town park one block east and one block south of the square. Children, teens and adults masqueraded in homemade costumes. In those Depression years no one ever thought of *buying* a costume. Excited giggling ghosts in bed sheets lined up along with a scarecrow in a tattered straw hat. A hobo in raggedy overalls and plaid shirt sported a corncob pipe and carried a bandana bundle on a stick over his shoulder. A horse with human feet, hobbyhorse head and rope tail wore a blanket covering it from its bumpy shoulders to its misshapen rear.

Verna was about a month old when Daddy announced that we were going to dress up and march in the Halloween Parade. And we were going to claim the top prize of ten dollars, a huge amount to us. We would go as an African-American family, he said. Only he didn't say "African-American." That term hadn't been thought of yet. He said the N-word, which was how everyone we knew referred to black folks in those days.

We rubbed our faces and hands with lard and blackened them with coal soot. Mama tied a big red bandana around her head and wore a print dress and apron. Daddy wore bib overalls and a work shirt and carried a hoe. Wilfred, Arden and Howard wore shirts and overalls, with stocking caps covering their blond hair. Carol and I, in print dresses, wore bandanas to cover our red hair.

In her wicker baby carriage, baby sister Verna was wrapped in a flannel blanket and wore a crocheted bonnet to cover her bald head. Mama said absolutely no to the idea of smearing coal soot on the baby's face and hands! When people peered into the baby buggy and remarked about the baby's white skin, Daddy told them that black babies are born with white skin and don't turn dark until they are at least six weeks old. Since no black people lived in Wakarusa, no one disputed his explanation.

We were quite a convincing family group. As Daddy predicted, we walked away with the coveted grand prize.

⇒ 23 ⇐

Doctors and Dentists

In fourth grade I saw the inside of a doctor's office for the first and only time in my childhood. A roller-skating accident in front of our house precipitated the visit.

One of my skates caught on an uneven crack in the sidewalk, and I went down hard. My right hand took the brunt of the impact. I was sure my wrist was broken. Through the throbbing pain and swelling, I secretly hoped it was. I would feel so important going to school with my right arm in a sling and my wrist in a cast. Everyone would be asking, "What happened?" and I would get to tell my story of the sidewalk rising up and slamming into my wrist.

Mama listened to hours of my moans and complaints, hoping and praying my wrist would get better without seeing a doctor. There was no money for a doctor. My wrist kept on hurting, and I kept on crying, until she gave in and took me to see Dr. Amick. His office was just around the corner from our house in the middle of town. We lived on Elkhart Street a half-block north of the stoplight, where s bank now stands, and Dr. Amick's office was on Waterford Street a half-block east of the stoplight.

Without x-rays, Dr. Amick determined that my injury was a sprain and not a fracture. He splinted and wrapped it and sent me home with my arm in a sling. I felt very important. Miss Searer, usually stern and serious, softened a little and made allowances for my illegible left-handed writing. In art class I even tried drawing with my left hand.

In seventh grade I saw a dentist for the first time in my life. Not Dr. Shoemaker, the town dentist and father of Bobby Shoemaker who was in my grade at school. A dentist from Elkhart (or maybe Goshen) came to our school and conducted a dental clinic. He did oral exams in a mobile dental office parked beside the school. I had twelve cavities, and was referred to Dr. Shoemaker to have them filled. I don't know who paid Dr. Shoemaker.

The visiting dentist presented an assembly program on dental health and how to clean and care for our teeth. He showed how to brush the lower teeth upward from the gums and the upper teeth downward from the gums, not back and forth as most children do, and to brush the inner as well as the outer surfaces. I never forgot his instructions. For more than sixty-five years I have practiced brushing my teeth the way he showed us, and it has paid off. I have no dentures to contend with. Bridges and crown aplenty, but no dentures.

Since then I've seen more doctors and dentists than I can count. I carry a list of my current ones in my wallet, along with lists of medications and emergency contacts. Around my neck I wear a Life Alert pendant, and in my purse I carry an emergency cell phone. Thanks to doctors and dentists, and the grace of God, I'm well on my way toward my goal of living to age one hundred.

24

Family Constellation

I am the first of seven children born during a span of twelve years. My parents were teenagers when I made my appearance in June of 1928. Mama turned sixteen three days before my birth, and Daddy had turned eighteen in March.

Three brothers and a sister came in quick succession during the next six years: Wilfred in January 1930, Arden in October 1931, Howard in February 1933, and Carol in August 1934. After Carol there was a gap of four years until Verna's arrival in September 1938 and then Sonja in December 1940. Mama had her hands full and then some.

Wilfred was hyper and mischievous. He loved to tease and torment, and sometimes he nearly drove Mama crazy. Today he would probably be diagnosed with ADHD, but we had never heard the term. Perhaps it hadn't been invented yet.

By the time Arden came along in October the year I was three, we had moved out of Grandpa and Grandma Gall's cramped apartment to the little gray house in the marsh. Mama said Arden was always hungry and crying for his next feeding. At the table he would cry for the next mouthful before she could get a single bite for herself.

Howard came next, born in February when I was five and a half and we lived north of Ligonier. He was cute as a button and turned out to be the smartest one in our family (and there wasn't a dull one among us). In second grade he won a reading contest, sailing through more than fifty books. His third grade teacher promoted him to fifth grade and gave me the responsibility of tutoring him in fourth grade arithmetic during summer vacation. It was an impossible assignment, as Howard refused to ruin a perfectly good summer with schoolwork.

Carol made her appearance in August the summer I turned six. One morning there she was in the cradle when we went into Mama's bedroom. I was thrilled to have a baby sister. When I asked where she came from, Mama said the doctor brought her. When our cow had a calf that same year, Mama told me Bossy had found it by a fence in the pasture field.

Mama was now twenty-two and Daddy was twenty-four. He worked as a farmhand for twenty dollars a month and a place to live. The Depression was nearing its midway point and would last another six or seven years.

When Wilfred and I needed shoes that winter, Mama and Daddy decided the only way they could buy shoes for us was to go without buying groceries for a month. They would get by with milk and butter from our cow, eggs from our chickens, potatoes and onions and canned tomatoes from the cellar, and whatever was on hand in the pantry. When that month ended, Daddy said he never wanted to eat potato soup again as long as he lived. Mama's potato soup with rivels was a huge favorite with all of us, and he ate lots of it while professing not to like it.

Verna was born in September when I was in fifth grade. This time Mama prepared me for the new baby's arrival by telling me the truth about where babies come from (their Mama's belly), but not a word about how they got in there. That piece of information came much later, and not from Mama.

I went to school that morning with a thrill of excitement and announced to my teacher, Mr. Anglemyer, that we had a new baby at our house. I wondered why he seemed less than surprised, and not at all excited at this news.

Mama had prepared for the new baby's arrival by having a big box built to hold blankets, diapers and baby clothes. We always called it the "baby box," even when there was no longer a baby in the house and the box was used for storing other things.

When Daddy brought the cradle downstairs and placed it in their bedroom, Carol asked if she could sleep in it. "Not tonight," Mama told her—and next morning there was the new baby in the cradle. Carol never did get to sleep in it.

Sonja, the youngest, was born on Christmas night when I was twelve. From a bedroom upstairs I listened through the stovepipe hole to Mama's moans and groans in the downstairs bedroom, heard the doctor arrive, and heard the baby utter her first cry. It was after midnight, and Daddy was disappointed that she didn't arrive on Christmas Day. The weather was rainy instead of snowy that year, and he always said with a chuckle that Santa was late getting there because he got stuck in the mud. He proudly named his newest daughter Sonja, after Olympic skater Sonja Henie.

By now, Mama was twenty-eight and Daddy was thirty. With seven children, their family was complete. The nine of us would have over-flowed today's seven-passenger minivans, but somehow we all managed to get into one six-passenger car, packed in like sardines.

I don't know what Mama and Daddy did to stop their family from growing still larger. Birth control pills did not come along until years later. I do remember once finding a strange round object in the bathroom and asking Mama what it was. She grabbed it out of my hand without an explanation, and I never saw it again.

As the big sister, I had the responsibility at an early age of helping with my younger siblings. They must have regarded me as their obnoxious, bossy big sister, but none of them ever threw that in my face once we became adults. I tried hard to please our parents and do what was right, and I tried to make my brothers behave too, but nobody could do that.

Left to right: Mama, Daddy, Shirley, Howard,
Carol, Wilfred, Verna, Arden, Sonja.

≈ 25 ≈

Places We Lived

At last count, I've lived in about fifty different places in my lifetime.

I began life in an apartment on Main Street in Nappanee, where we lived with Grandpa and Grandma Gall and Aunt Kathryn, Uncle Bud, his wife Violet and their son Richard, six months younger than I. After Wilfred's birth the apartment became too crowded. It was time for us to move.

We moved to the little gray house in the marsh in the spring of 1930. The U.S. Census record of April 4, 1930, shows us living there, in Union Township, and Francis M. and Anna E. Mitchell (Pa and Ma) living nearby.

Arden was born in the little gray house in October 1931. Before Howard's arrival in February 1933 we had moved again, to a house on State Road 5 north of Ligonier. And by the time Carol arrived in August of 1934 we had moved to the Smith farm southwest of Ligonier. This is where we lived when I started first grade at Perry School. The Smith place is memorable for its round barn where the cows were stanchioned, fed and milked in a circle facing the center.

Our next move was to Edwardsburg, Michigan, where we lived in a little gray house on Redfield Road (a house that now sports blue vinyl siding). I finished first grade and started second grade at Edwardsburg Elementary School. That fall (1935) we moved in with Grandma Miller south of Nappanee for a few weeks and I attended a one-room country school where most of the students were Amish. This is where I trudged two miles to school and two miles home, in the snow, and it was uphill both ways. (Just kidding.)

The week after Christmas we moved to Wakarusa, which became our hometown from that time on. Our first home in Wakarusa was the Smeltzer house one block south and one block west of the square. Next was a house "uptown," a half-block north of the square, where we lived when I was in fourth grade, next-door to Faye Ryan and her brother Lester. Before I started fifth grade we moved to the Grove house two blocks west and a block south of the square. Verna was born there in the fall of 1938.

Here Daddy raised hogs in a lot enclosed by an electric fence. Four-year-old Carol took hold of the fence one day and could not let go, her muscles paralyzed by the electric current until someone turned off the power. One of Daddy's hogs was less fortunate. It bit the fence and was electrocuted.

Our next move was to the Harter house four miles north and a mile and a half west of town. This is where Sonja made her appearance on the day after Christmas in 1940, when I was in seventh grade.

Before the next December we moved to the Lechlitner place, another little gray house. This is where we lived when Pearl Harbor was bombed in December 1941. Mama and Daddy brought home an "extra" edition of the *Elkhart Truth* with a headline in four-inch type. We lived at the Lechlitner place for most of World War II.

The winter of 1944-45 we moved to the house on Osborne Road that became our family home for the next three decades. It was the first and only home that Daddy and Mama ever owned.

Osborne Road was the twelfth place we had lived by the time I finished high school. After leaving the family home I lived in another thirty or more places – in Elkhart and Mishawaka, Indiana; Share and Jos, Nigeria; Pasadena, Monrovia, Lakewood and Los Angeles in Southern California; Cassopolis, Michigan; South Bend, Indiana; Okeechobee, Florida, and Wilmore, Kentucky.

The longest I ever lived in one place was twelve and a half years (1977 to 1989) in our house on Greenwood Avenue in Los Angeles. The shortest was one month in an apartment on Centinela Avenue in Los Angeles, just after Bill and I were married.

I moved into my home on Brookwood Lane in Wilmore in June 1999, eight years ago as I write this. Here is where I hope to live until I move to my permanent dwelling place, a mansion in the sky.

26

A Place of Their Own

Daddy and Mama had dreamed for years of having a place of their own, a house and a piece of land in the country. The dream looked utterly impossible. It took everything Daddy earned just to pay the rent, buy food and clothing and shoes for seven kids, and gas and tires for a car to transport us. Accumulating enough money for a down payment looked unattainable.

Their impossible dream came true in the winter of 1944-45, thanks to the generosity and trust of Ira Brown, who owned an old house and considerable acreage in St. Joseph County. The house sat on a 27-acre parcel on the southwest corner of Osborne Road and Ash Road (Elkhart County Line). The road separated the parcel from the rest of his acreage.

Mr. Brown had watched the Gall family and observed how Thurlo and Nora worked hard and always paid their bills. In the seven years since they first showed up in Wakarusa, they had proved themselves honorable and trustworthy. He thought they ought to have a chance at home ownership, and agreed to sell the house with its twenty-seven acres at a reasonable price and favorable terms.

During Christmas vacation in 1944 we began the big job of cleaning and refurbishing the house before moving in. We washed and painted woodwork, removed old wallpaper, hung new wallpaper, cleaned the sagging floors, washed windows and hung curtains. Wilfred and I stayed in our "new" house part of that time, to keep the fire going in the stove and continue the cleaning and wallpaper removal. I'm not sure how much we accomplished on our own. In the attic we found some fascinating old books and papers that distracted us from the work at hand.

The house had three rooms downstairs: living room, bedroom, and a lean-to kitchen. The kitchen windows looked out across the fields to the south. Steep wooden stairs with no landing led from the living room to the dirt-floor basement, which could also be entered by outside steps under slanting double cellar doors.

The small first-floor bedroom had once been two, even smaller, rooms. A steep wooden staircase led from the bedroom to the second floor and opened into one of the four small rooms upstairs. The floors up there sagged even more than the ones downstairs. The best set of stairs in the house led to a big attic with wide bare floorboards that were solid and sturdy. The only closet in the entire house was the space under the attic stairs.

A wood-burning stove in the living room heated the house, and Mama cooked on a wood-burning range in the kitchen. We pumped water by hand from the well outside the kitchen door. At night we read, played games and did homework by the light of kerosene lamps. In one corner of the back yard stood the outhouse, about fifty feet from the kitchen door. In the other corner stood a shed and corncrib.

We moved in sometime in January or February. With only two or three months remaining until school ended in April, we hoped to complete the school year at Wakarusa. We could board the bus at the County Line Road close to our house, and transfer to Madison School in the fall. The Olive Township trustee denied permission, saying we had to live in the township in order to attend school in Wakarusa. However, if we and at least one parent physically slept in the township, we could go to school there.

Ira Brown owned a vacant house on the corner opposite ours, in Olive Township. He agreed to allow Daddy and the six of who were in school to sleep there for the duration of the school year, while Mama and Sonja slept in our house on Osborne Road.

The house on Osborne Road became our family home, and is still the place we think of as home. Daddy and Mama made many improvements over the years, including an indoor bathroom, modernized

84

kitchen, garage and workroom annex, and concrete front porch, patio and driveway.

I think Daddy's pride and joy, though, was his barn, with cattle stalls and space for raising hogs. His dream of creating a lake on the property never materialized. Daddy died in his barn from a sudden heart attack on September 6, 1970, while he was busy tending his animals.

⇒ 27 ⇐

Daddy

Daddy loved his little farm on Osborne Road. He made his living on the railroad, but he lived his life on the farm.

Wherever we'd lived before that, even in town, he had nearly always managed to keep a cow and some chickens, even pigs. Now, for the first time, he had land of his own. Twenty-seven acres to pasture his animals and raise field crops. He built a barn for his animals. He bought a tractor to work his fields. He was in his glory when he had a grandchild or two trailing him, riding with him on the tractor, or on the wagon helping him shuck corn.

He watched the signs and seasons to know whether the coming winter would be mild or severe. He watched the birds and insects and animals as weather predictors. He knew the best time to plant potatoes and wheat and corn, and the best times for harvesting. He noted when the birds flew south and when they returned.

He enjoyed seeing the purple martins swooping in and out of the martin house on a tall pole in the back yard. He loved to watch them building their nests, raising their young and catching gazillions of mosquitoes over a summer. He delighted in watching a pair of robins build their nest and raise their young at eye level in the linden tree outside the kitchen window.

When I was seven, Daddy showed me how to pull a towel back and forth to dry my back. He sensed that it was no longer appropriate for him to dry me off after my Saturday night bath. I still think of him when I dry my back after a shower, and appreciate his sensitivity to my growing sense of self.

We moved to Wakarusa the winter of 1935 because Daddy had landed a job at Vesey's greenhouse on East Waterford Street. One cold winter night he let me stay with him while he stoked the furnace to keep the greenhouses warm. I felt special because he wanted me to keep him company, and important because he let me help sort gladiolus bulbs. Safe and secure with my big, strong Daddy, I fell asleep long before midnight and was not much company for him.

Daddy's next job was at Weaver's Hatchery next door to the greenhouse, and after that he worked a while for the WPA. While he was working on the WPA, he and Uncle Toby entered the Golden Gloves amateur boxing tournament in Elkhart. I don't think he had ever boxed before, but he was willing to try most anything, if only for the fun of it. His effort got our family's picture in the *Elkhart Truth*.

Family Support for Wakarusa Finalist

HEAVYWEIGHT THURLO GALL of Wakarusa, 29-year-old WPA worker, will have plenty of support in his Golden Glove title bout tonight at the EHS gymnasium. He is pictured here with his family, left to right, as follows: Arden, age 8; Mrs. Gall, holding Marlene, age 1; Mr. Gall holding Carol, age 5; Howard, age 7; Shirley, age 11; and Wilfred, age 16. (TRUTH PHOTO).

Family Support, Elkhart Truth Photo

His next job was working for Russ Thompson as a farmhand, and also at Russ's dead animal rendering plant. That was one workplace I didn't care to visit with Daddy. He always came home from work covered from head to toe with gray dust and smelling like dead animals. Without a bathroom, I don't know how he ever got washed clean enough to get into bed with Mama, but he must have. Sonja was born on that farm in the house we called the Harter place.

After the start of World War II and the rationing of gasoline and tires, Daddy bought a Harley-Davidson motorcycle to ride to and from his foundry job at Adams and Westlake in Elkhart. He learned to ride his motorcycle despite the fact that he had never learned to ride a bicycle. I felt so cool when he would give me a ride on his motorcycle to someplace I needed to go.

Mama felt less than cool the day he tried to ride up the bank of Willy Lechlitner's lawn, from a standing position on the road, with her on the seat behind him. Without the necessary momentum, the motorcycle stalled and fell over. Mama's ankle was broken and she spent a night or two in the hospital.

One weekend Daddy and Mama rode the motorcycle to visit Uncle Harve in Henry, Illinois, where he was doing alternative service as a conscientious objector. On the way home Daddy fell asleep and ran off the road. He suffered a concussion, but Mama had no serious injuries. She walked to a nearby house to get help, and the neighbor brought them home. I don't remember how they got the motorcycle home. Daddy seemed not to know where he was or what had happened, and I worried that he would never be "right" again. It was a huge relief when he returned to his senses after a few days.

Daddy's next job, as a brakeman on the New York Central Railroad, was the one he held for the rest of his life, from about 1943 to 1970. He was on call at all hours of the day and night and had to catch his sleep while he was home, even if it was bright daylight. The rest of us had to be as quiet as possible so he could get his rest, and listen for the telephone call summoning him to his next run. That call could sometimes come after only eight hours off.

When I was living at Share in Nigeria, I dreamed one night that Daddy and Mama came for a visit. I was so excited to see them drive into the mission compound, round the circular driveway and stop in front of the mission house where I lived. When John and Betty Bontrager came back to Share from their furlough in Indiana, they brought a tape with a message for me from Daddy. He cried as he told me, "Daughter, I miss you so much. Sometimes I can hardly stand it." I cried when I listened to him crying.

After Bill and I were married in Pasadena we spent part of our honeymoon on the farm in Indiana. Daddy and Mama hosted a wedding reception for us on their beautiful green lawn. Friends, neighbors and relatives came to wish us well. All too soon it was time to say goodbye and head back west. Gene Huff and Jack Harrington drove us to O'Hare Airport to catch a plane back to Los Angeles.

As we drove away, Daddy and Mama stood on the front porch of the house on Osborne Road, surrounded by grandchildren and waving goodbye. The scene is a living photograph forever etched in my mind. It was the last time I saw Daddy alive.

Still in love after 35 years, 1963

28

Monster in the House

Mama sewed and mended our clothes on an old Domestic treadle sewing machine that was already ancient when she was born in 1912. It had belonged to her Grandma Slabaugh, who died when I was a preschooler. I have a dim memory of seeing her laid out in her Amish home, and lots of people coming in and out. They all spoke Pennsylvania Dutch, and as they arrived, each person went around the room greeting everyone with a handshake.

It must have been about that time that Mama acquired her Grandma's sewing machine and began her love-hate relationship with the black monster that was noisy as a freight train and stubborn as a mule. Sometimes it would cooperate and produce a beautiful seam. Sometimes it produced only snarls and knots and loops of thread where they didn't belong.

That old treadle sewing machine had come equipped with a box of attachments in one of its drawers, and a little instruction book telling how to use them. Mama never tried to use the attachments. It was hard enough just getting the cantankerous old beast to sew a simple seam with the top and bottom tension matching. As a little girl I played with the attachments, and later I learned to sew on that noisy old machine.

After World War II money became a little less scarce and electricity came to the farm. Mama bought a brand-new Kenmore electric sewing machine in an oak-veneer cabinet that doubled as a desk and made a handsome addition to our living room. The new machine hummed like a top and made sewing a delight.

Mama lost no time getting rid of the old Domestic monster. She had Daddy haul it off to the dump where it joined the South Bend Malleable wood-burning cook stove in a rusty grave. Mama had no idea that her old "junk" items were valuable antiques.

I've often wished that I had that old treadle sewing machine. It would command a place of honor in my home.

⇐ 29 ⇒

Deadly Silence

Silence was a deadly weapon in our family.

Daddy and Mama used it when they were upset with each other. They could go for a whole week or two without speaking, and we usually didn't have a clue about what had brought on their silent battle. When one or the other had had enough of the silent treatment, the battle would end and they would speak and act as if nothing had happened.

Mama told me once that when she asked Daddy what he'd been mad about, he said, "Mad? I'm not the one who was mad."

Mama was known to use the silent treatment on other people as well. During Sonja's senior year in high school, Mama was upset about something (I never knew what) and not speaking to her. When it came time for the Mother-Daughter Tea, she was still not speaking to Sonja. I went to the tea in Mama's place rather than have Sonja go alone.

In our family we had arguments but not discussions. We were not allowed to express our feelings. "Pouting" or "back-talk" got us sent to our room without supper. There the anger would seethe and build up inside us.

In the extended Gall family it seemed that someone was always "on the outs" with the rest of the family over some real or imagined offense. If Grandma Gall was not speaking to someone, the rest of us were supposed to give him or her the silent treatment too.

After Pa Mitchell died, Ma Mitchell went to New York City to stay with her daughter, Sue Callahan, Grandma Gall's sister. We knew her as Aunt Sue. I never found out whether Ma Mitchell went to New York City because Grandma Gall (Viola) was not speaking to her, or Viola was not speaking to her because she went to New York. At any rate, they were not on speaking terms when Ma Mitchell died in New York. At the funeral and burial, Grandma Gall cried and wailed inconsolably. It was too late to make amends and too late to say, "I'm sorry."

I was in Nigeria when Grandpa Gall (Frank) died. Grandma Gall sent me pictures and wrote that when he lay dying she called for Babe (Daddy) to come and say goodbye, but he refused. Babe and Nora were not speaking to Grandma and Grandpa. So far as I know, they never again spoke to her.

When I visited Grandma Gall after I came home from Nigeria, she was grieving over the long silence. She showed me a pair of Grandpa Gall's nice leather house slippers and wanted me to take them to Daddy. I'm ashamed that I did not take them to him and encourage him to make peace with his mother. As a mother and grandmother I know now what a grievous thing it is when children and grandchildren cut off communication.

The fact is, I was afraid. I didn't know what had caused the rift, and I didn't know how to be a mediator. I missed an opportunity to at least try to bring reconciliation. Grandma Gall died six years later with the silence still unbroken and the rift unmended. I didn't know whether Daddy and Mama would even show up at her funeral, and I was afraid to ask if they were going. Imagine that. Afraid to mention it to them! If I broached the subject, would they be mad at me and give me the silent treatment too?

Years later I did venture to ask Mama why Daddy didn't go say goodbye to his dying father. She said they'd had so many false alarms they thought this was another one and just didn't go.

The silent treatment showed up again between Aunt Sis (Edith) and her daughter Marilyn. According to Marilyn, it started over a matter of drawing names for Christmas and escalated when someone failed to show up for Christmas dinner. The season of love and peace and goodwill became a season of bad will and they never spoke to each other again. When Aunt Sis died and Marilyn stood at her mother's casket in the funeral parlor, her father stood beside her and snarled, "Why are you here? You didn't bother to speak to her when she was alive."

And so the silence goes on hurting generation after generation. It kills relationships and distorts truth until no one knows what started it all. It pursues loved ones to the grave, and then it's too late to end the deadly silence.

PART 2

Launching Out

New horizons, new opportunities

⇒ 30 ⇐

College on a Prayer and a Shoestring

In the history of our entire family, Aunt Kathryn was the first I know of to graduate from high school. In the spring of 1946 I became the second.

On Mama's side of the family, education beyond eighth grade was prohibited as vain and worldly. The Amish hold that higher education leads to a desire to be like the world and would threaten their way of life. A high school diploma and a college degree are not necessary for the pursuit of their plain and simple lifestyle as farmers and skilled artisans.

Education held little importance for the Gall family either. They had no religious teaching against it, but most of them were farmers and blue-collar workers with no need for higher learning.

I don't know where the idea came from, but all through high school I knew that I would go to college. The only question was where and how. Every summer at camp meeting I visited the Christian college displays and talked to representatives from Marion College, Taylor University, Fort Wayne Bible Institute and Kentucky Mountain Bible College. I picked up all their brochures, took them home and dreamed, wondering which would be the best place for me and how I would pay for a college education.

I knew my parents struggled to make ends meet and I could not count on them for help. In fact, I would not even dream of asking. I knew nothing about college scholarships, grants or loans. If they were available, no one ever told me.

When the Missionary Church (Mennonite Brethren in Christ at that time) decided to open a college in Mishawaka only twenty miles from our home on Osborne Road, that settled the question of where I would go. The how would come about by working to pay my own way.

After graduating from high school in the spring of 1946, I went to work on an assembly line at CTS in Elkhart and saved every

Shirley, high school graduation, 1946

penny I could for college. My job was assembling springs and cams in radio switches, a task so repetitive that I could do it with my eyes closed, and so boring that I sometimes fell asleep. When the inspector at the end of the line found switches with springs and cams incorrectly assembled, I became the chief suspect and received a warning from the line boss. After that, my coworkers kept a jar of smelling salts and waved it under my nose whenever they saw me nodding.

Bethel College opened in the fall of 1947, and I enrolled in its first freshman class. Of the 93 students registered that first year, I was number 71.

Since my pre-teen years I had felt called to serve God as a missionary in some far corner of the earth. Which corner was not clear, but I was sure God would show me where if I was obedient to him. Enrolling at Bethel College was a first step of obedience to that call.

That fall I was hired for a part-time office job at Ball Band, a large footwear manufacturer in Mishawaka. To make it possible for students to work in the afternoon, the college scheduled most classes in the morning. Monday through Friday, many of us hurried through lunch, boarded a bus to Ball Band, worked four hours and returned to campus in time for supper. Evenings and weekends I often did babysitting, ironing or cleaning for additional income.

Just before the end of my freshman year, I landed in the hospital with my left leg shattered at the knee and needing surgery to repair it. I took my final exams in the hospital and spent the summer sidelined and unable to work, with a cast from toes to thigh. Students and faculty took a collection to help pay my hospital bill, but the surgeon's bill still had to be paid.

In September the cast was off, but I was still on crutches. I returned to college with a prayer for God to supply my needs. The college gave me a job at the switchboard, and I worked out a payment plan with Dr. Friedman. As soon as I could walk without crutches I went back to work at Ball Band, where I worked for the rest of my college years. By living frugally, working twenty hours a week during the school year and full-time during winter and summer breaks, I was managing to pay my way.

Then, in the middle of my third year in college, I suffered another broken leg, just above my right ankle. This time a manager in the Ball Band sales department arranged for the Red Cross to pay my hospital and doctors' bills. As soon as I was able to get around on crutches, I was back in classes, back at work, and back singing in the choir. I participated in local concerts, but had to miss the spring concert tour.

Five years after beginning college, I received my bachelor's degree in Biblical Literature in 1952. In those five years I had received less than a hundred dollars in assistance with my school bills, but prayer and a shoestring had brought me through. I graduated debt-free.

══ 31 ══

A Walk in the Woods

On a Sunday afternoon in May, near the end of my freshman year in college, two friends from town dropped by my dorm for a visit. Enticed by spring sunshine, we went for a walk in the beautiful oak woods behind the dorms.

Our path led us near "the glen," a deep natural hollow filled with uprooted tree stumps. Those proud oaks had stood for decades in these woods. Now the basement of the administration building had displaced them, and their trunks had become lumber for the floors of dorms and faculty homes. From the bottom of the glen their massive roots reached upward like giant grasping hands.

The trees on the rim of the hollow stood like sentinels mourning their fallen brothers. A rope tied to a limb of one tree beckoned and invited us to swing out over the glen. I had seen some of the young men swinging on the rope, and it looked like great fun. I had to try it. Grabbing the rope above its knotted end, I swung out and back. My friends tried it too. It was fun.

Growing bolder, I tried swinging in an arc as I had seen some of the guys do, instead of straight out and back. Longer ride, more fun—until I failed to get my footing on the return. The rope's momentum began to carry me out again, and I knew I could not hold on long enough for another return. I let go near the bank to avoid landing on those menacing tree roots below.

The moment I hit the ground I knew my left leg was broken. It was bent nearly ninety degrees to the left at the knee. One of my friends stayed with me while the other ran for help. A crowd soon gathered.

A fire department rescue team arrived to take me to St. Joseph Hospital in Mishawaka. But first they yanked my leg hard to straighten it enough to get me onto a stretcher. I nearly passed out. On the ride to the hospital, every bump and vibration brought fresh stabs of pain and surges of moaning and crying.

My friend Evelyn, riding in the ambulance with me, tried to lighten me up a little.

"Just think of the excitement you're creating," she said above the siren's blare. "Everybody's watching and wondering what happened."

The emergency room doctor called in an orthopedic surgeon.

"You will need surgery to repair the damage," said the surgeon, Dr. Friedman. "Otherwise you will have a stiff knee joint for the rest of your life. We'll put a temporary cast on today, and schedule the surgery for Wednesday." He yanked on my leg to straighten it further before encasing it in plaster.

In the emergency room an angel of mercy showed up to hold my hand and comfort me. Joan Culp had been my friend since second grade, and we had graduated together from Wakarusa High School two years ago. Now she was in nurses' training in this hospital.

All that night I moaned with pain as my leg swelled inside the cast. No amount of morphine helped. In the morning, when the doctor sawed the cast open to relieve the pressure, my bruised and discolored flesh nearly overflowed the opening. Daddy broke into tears when he saw it that afternoon after returning from a run on the railroad.

The three days until the surgery on Wednesday seemed interminable. Then came sixteen more days in the hospital. After all that time immobilized in bed and in a wheelchair, I couldn't wait to get up and walk when Mama arrived with the crutches the doctor had ordered. But as soon as I tried to stand upright, I blacked out and fell back onto the bed. So much for walking out of the hospital.

A quiet Sunday afternoon in May turned into a long hot summer in a hip-to-toe cast.

I wish I could say that I learned never again to take foolish risks, but I can't. I've needed rescue from numerous perils, some beyond my control, but many of my own making. It's been a busy sixty years for my guardian angel.

∽ 32 ∾

Saying Goodbye

A crescent moon hung in the November sky as I waited for the Twentieth Century Limited that would carry me overnight from Elkhart to Grand Central Station in New York. The first leg of a five-week journey to Nigeria, West Africa, was about to begin. Surrounded by family and friends, I felt excited yet apprehensive about the new life I was embarking on.

I looked forward to learning a new language, confident that I would astound everyone by my quick grasp of vocabulary, grammar and pronunciation. I had just completed a three-month course at the Summer Institute of Linguistics in Grand Forks, North Dakota, and was eager to apply what I had learned about learning a language.

From childhood I had been watching slide shows of life in faraway mission fields as missionaries visited our church, told of their adventures and displayed exotic artifacts. I was already planning how I would impress audiences as a missionary on furlough. But first I had to say goodbye to my family and to the good and loving people from my church. They were all there at the Elkhart train station to bid me farewell. There must have been a hundred people gathered around me as I waited to board.

The big diesel engine with its line of sleek passenger cars arrived right on time. The conductor leaned out between two cars and placed a step stool on the ground. Arriving passengers exited and were met by waiting loved ones. The conductor called "All aboard," and departing passengers began boarding.

I waited until everyone else had boarded, putting off as long as possible the moment of saying goodbye. What would it be like to be an ocean and a continent away? Not to see my family or any of these friends for three years or more? Not hear their voices? To wait two or three months for letters from home?

Shirley off to Nigeria

The moment came, and I could not put it off any longer. I had to mount that step and get on the train and wave goodbye to all of them. I would be brave. I would not cry.

My resolve melted as that crowd of family and friends sang to me: "God be with you till meet again; by his mercy guide, uphold you; with his sheep securely fold you; God be with you till we meet again." The tears began flowing.

"Till we meet, till we meet, till we meet at Jesus' feet…" The trickle became a flood. What if our next meeting *were* to be at Jesus' feet? What if this were the last time I would see any of them on this earth?

It was time for the conductor to close the doors. I entered the car to my right and made my way down the aisle to an empty seat. The hard goodbye was over. A new part of my life was beginning. The new moon in the sky was my witness.

⟹ 33 ⟸

Next Steps

The United Missionary Society had accepted me in the spring of 1952 for service in Nigeria, but stipulated that I get at least a year of practical ministry experience before going overseas.

That summer I began working at the Cedar Road Missionary Church in Osceola. My job included secretarial work, visitation, leading children's church and a midweek teen group, directing Vacation Bible School, writing and directing the Christmas program, and teaching neighborhood Good News Clubs.

The following summer I attended Wycliffe's Summer Institute of Linguistics at the University of North Dakota in Grand Forks, to learn how to learn a language on the field.

We learned to describe and write down the sounds that appear in the world's thousands of languages, including our own. We learned how to hear and reproduce these sounds in a field setting, and the many ways of putting sounds together to form words and putting words together to form sentences. We learned that our usual subject-verb-object order in English grammar does not work in many other languages.

We learned about tonal languages, in which the pitch of a syllable or word is as significant as the combination of vowels and consonants. This was particularly helpful in learning the Nupe language, which has five significant tones: high, mid and low, plus an up glide and a down glide. Use the wrong tone, and it's a different word altogether. For instance, eba (mid-low) means yes, but eba (mid-high) means husband, and eba (mid-mid) means penis. Etsu (high-high) means chief, but etsu (mid-high) means rat! You can't be too careful about correct tonality.

A five-week boat trip landed me in Lagos, Nigeria, and an all-night ride in a lorry (a truck used for hauling both passengers and cargo) brought me to our mission headquarters in Ilorin. From there a mission car took me to Share (Tsaragi in Nupe), where I would spend my first year in Nigeria. Somehow my barrels and boxes got to Share too, but I don't remember how or when.

My frugal lifestyle during five years of college and my upbringing on a farm with an outdoor toilet and no electricity or running water, had prepared me well for life in Share. It had not prepared me for being rich in comparison to the local citizens.

Here I had a one-hole *indoor* toilet with a bucket to catch the deposits, and a laborer to carry the contents outside and bury them in the ground. On the mission compound we had a laborer to draw water from the compound well and fill the elevated water tanks outside our mission houses to give us running water for showers. He drew our water for drinking and cooking too, and then a cook or houseboy boiled it and filled the big filter jar. We used only boiled and filtered water for drinking and for washing and cooking our food.

A houseboy did my cooking and cleaning and laundry. The local women bathed and did their laundry in a muddy stream, then dipped water from the same stream and carried it home on their heads for cooking and drinking. They toiled in their gardens outside the town, ground their grain by hand on a flat stone, cooked their family's food in clay pots over open fires, and carried babies on their backs while going about their many tasks.

I slept in a bed with a mattress and a mosquito net. They slept on straw mats on the floor. I wore shoes to protect my feet from disease and injury. They went barefoot. Because I could read, I had a wealth of knowledge and information. They had no hope or knowledge of anything beyond their life of toil and tears.

People came and went all around me, all the time. Some families lived on the mission compound. Others came for medical treatment at the mission dispensary. They brought their malnourished children with distended bellies. They brought babies half-dead from fever and dehydration. They came with ulcerous sores on their guinea worm infested legs. Patients from a distance stayed in huts on the compound when they needed extended treatment. Family members stayed with them to prepare food and care for them.

A steady stream of people walked and rode bicycles past the mission compound, carrying incredibly heavy loads on their heads. Women walked from the town to toil in their fields. They came from their fields carrying loads of grain and produce on their heads, or from the water hole carrying heavy buckets of water. Men rode by on bicycles balancing bundles of ten-foot bamboo roofing poles or bundles of thatching grass on their heads.

I saw people everywhere, and yet I felt lonely and isolated, cut off from everything and everyone familiar. Mail delivery was infrequent. Letters from home were few and far between. I longed to see my family and friends back home in Indiana. I longed to talk and laugh with them like old times.

I wished for a place where I could go all by myself and pull out the stops. I wanted to scream and cry and pound on a tree without being heard, but I didn't dare to venture into the bush by myself. I was afraid of what I might encounter, and afraid of getting lost. One day I pulled out the stops at home in my little thatch-roofed house. I cried and moaned and pounded on my bed. Next morning our dear young student pastor, John Kolo, came to my door with a note for me. On a scrap of greeting-card paper he had written in pencil: "Soniya (my Nupe name), yesterday I heard you crying in your house, and I think that you are longed for your people. I will pray for you."

This simple message of empathy and comfort, written from the heart of a Nigerian brother, was to me a word from heaven, brought by the hand of a black-skinned angel named John. I have treasured that note and kept it in my Nupe Bible all these years.

In the year that I lived at Share I studied the Nupe language diligently, applying what I had learned at the Summer Institute of Linguistics. I hoped to impress everyone with my quick grasp of the language and my ability to communicate fluently. My attempts were often met with laughter from the locals, and it was hard to tell whether they were laughing with delight at my attempts to speak their language or with scorn because of my mistakes. On the whole they were kind and helpful though.

They laughed when I used the word for washing clothes (which means pounding) to describe washing my hair, then told me the right word to use. They laughed when I used the wrong word for husband, then told me how to say it with the right tones.

Before the end of the year I passed my Nupe language exam. At the field conference in November I was assigned to Rock Haven, our mission hostel at Jos. My job would be to help care for missionary kids and help to host missionaries coming for their annual month of rest and recuperation. I made the trip by train in early December and settled into a room in the guesthouse until the completion of a house for my friend, Marion Lehman, and me. She would be our UMS teacher on the staff of Hillcrest School where our children attended.

At Jos I would have no occasion to speak or hear Nupe, no opportunities to demonstrate my incredible grasp of vocabulary, pronunciation, grammar and syntax. I would be working and communicating in English and trying to pick up some Hausa, the trade language of the North. So much for impressing people with my language skills.

⇒ 34 ⇐

Adventures in Mission

G rowing up in the Wakarusa Missionary Church, I heard missionaries at church and camp meeting all the time. Their stories
captivated me. One missionary taught us "Jesus Loves Me" in Spanish;
another taught us "Bringing in the Sheaves" in Chinese. They showed
pictures and artifacts from the "foreign fields" where they served.

By the time I was ten or eleven I began to sense that God wanted
me to be a missionary and tell the good news of Jesus to people in a
foreign field. I didn't have a clear idea of how I would do that, but I
could see myself as a missionary on furlough telling stories of exciting
events, displaying artifacts from a faraway land, and showing slides of
exotic people and places.

In college I began *being* a missionary in "my Jerusalem," a trailer park
adjacent to the college campus. While living there for a summer, my
roommate and I felt a burden to reach out to the children. With permission from the park management, we conducted a Good News Club in
the laundry room. With other helpers I continued this ministry until
I graduated in June of 1952. I also did children's ministry at Liberty
Missionary Church near the campus. After graduation I worked full-
time for a year at Cedar Road Missionary Church in Osceola before
heading overseas.

In the spring of 1953, the United Missionary Society appointed me
to Nigeria. The Wakarusa Missionary Church took on my full support,

which amounted to $750 a year, and helped to outfit me with clothing and supplies for a three-year term.

That summer I attended the Summer Institute of Linguistics in North Dakota, and in November I began a five-week trip to Nigeria on a freighter. Most of the twelve passengers on board were missionaries. We reached Lagos two days before Christmas, and I arrived at Share, my assigned station, on December 31.

My assignment was to study the Nupe language and conduct a one-room school, in English, for eight children in first through third grades. At the end of that year I was assigned to help with the care of missionary children at Rock Haven in Jos and with hosting missionaries on their annual vacations (called holidays in Nigeria).

This was not the kind of missionary work I had anticipated, but I loved serving at Jos. I enjoyed helping to make a home away from home for missionary kids during their long months of separation from their moms and dads while attending school at Hillcrest. I also enjoyed hosting the missionaries as they came for rejuvenation in the cooler climate of the Bauchi Plateau.

After two and a half years in Jos I flew home for furlough in June of 1957, in time for my twenty-ninth birthday. On furlough my slides and artifacts were unimpressive, and I had no exciting tales to tell about exotic people and places. What I *could* tell people was that in loving and caring for missionary children, and ministering to missionaries on holiday, I was participating in all of their ministries. I was helping them to do what they were called to do: teaching, preaching, doctoring, nursing, evangelizing, and training workers.

At the end of my furlough year I was asked to work in the UMS home office in Elkhart, as secretary to the foreign secretary, Dick Reilly. I was his entire office staff. My job included booking missionary travel to and from the fields, scheduling mission conferences, producing a 16-page monthly magazine, *The Missionary Banner,* and running the office for extended periods when Dick was out of the country. One of his out-of-the-country stints lasted a year and a half—and this was decades before the advent of satellite phones, personal computers, email and instant communication worldwide.

With Dick's blessing, and with a letter of recommendation from him to his friend Ted Engstrom, I was invited to join the publication staff of World Vision International in Southern California. In January 1966 I loaded all my earthly possessions into and on top of my 1955 Chevy and drove 2400 miles to Los Angeles. I left Indiana in a snowstorm and drove into summery California sunshine. My new job began on February 1.

California, here I come!

Dr. Engstrom, World Vision's executive vice-president, welcomed me to the editorial staff of *World Vision Magazine* and *World Vision Scope.* The sign on my door said "Copy Editor." I adopted the unofficial title of "Chief Nitpicker" to describe my responsibility for proofreading every piece of printed material World Vision published. I was good at what I did, and very few errors escaped my eagle eye—with one notable exception to keep me humble. A letter to donors from Ted Engstrom went to print, *after* I'd proofread it, with the complimentary closing "Gratefully yours" spelled g-r-e-a-t-f-u-l-l-y!

While working at World Vision I met Bill McMillan in the single adult group at Lake Avenue Congregational Church in Pasadena. He worked in aerospace and had long been active with the Navigators and in a workplace Bible Club ministry.

After our marriage I continued to be involved with World Vision as a volunteer. I placed donation boxes in local businesses, collected and counted donations, and forwarded a monthly check to help World Vision relieve hunger. At our church in West Los Angeles, Bill and I served together on the Missions Committee, and later on the International Friendship Committee.

With thousands of international students streaming to Los Angeles to study, we literally had "the world at our doorstep." We initiated friendships with some of the first students coming to UCLA from Mainland China. We invited them to our home, planned special events and trips, and shared the love of Jesus with internationals from many countries.

Our small home had only two bedrooms, but when our son, Jimmy, was no longer living at home, we used the second bedroom to host students from all over the world, who came to study at the English Language School in Santa Monica. They lived in our home for a month or two, and sometimes longer. We provided room and board at ELS's established rate and helped our guests with English conversation and American customs and culture. We tried to live the gospel before them every day, and we shared the gospel with words at every opportunity.

At church, Bill served as commander of the Christian Service Brigade and I chaired the Pioneer Girls Committee and led the middlers Sunday school department. We also led discipleship groups using the Navigators' 2:7 Series, based on Colossians 2:6-7, *"So then, just as you received Christ Jesus as Lord, continue to live in him, rooted and built up in him, strengthened in the faith as you were taught, and overflowing with thankfulness."*

When we moved to South Bend after Bill's retirement, we immediately signed on with the Friendship Family program at the University of Notre Dame. Our first of many contacts was Yangshi Gu from China. When he came to our home for the first time and we sat down to the dinner table, Bill began to explain that we are Christians and it's our custom to give thanks to God for our food. Before he could finish the sentence, Yangshi announced, "I am almost a Christian!" And he was. He'd been attending a Bible study on campus and was almost ready to make a decision. Before a year went by we had the joy of witnessing his baptism. He was the first of many Christian Chinese students in our lives.

One of the first things I did when I moved to Wilmore, Kentucky in 1999 was to get in touch with the Office of International Student Services at Asbury Theological Seminary. I started befriending internationals, inviting them to meals in my home, helping them with English conversation and editing their papers for clarity and correct English usage. And I joined the International Friendship Team at Wilmore Free Methodist Church.

In August of 2000 a small announcement in the church bulletin caught my attention. It said that a pastor from Florida needed room and board for the seminary's fall semester. Though I had not planned to take in boarders, I sensed that I should call the number listed. I called the next day and learned that the pastor was a Haitian living in Florida, and that he had a wife and three children who would remain in Florida. He had completed all but one year at the ATS Orlando campus and needed to come to Wilmore for his final year. Five days later I met Yvan Pierre at the bus station in Lexington and brought him to live in my home for what turned out to be two semesters and the January term.

During that year our hearts bonded as he shared with me his passion for Haiti to be transformed by the power of Jesus Christ. He had already begun a fledgling ministry called International Christian Development Mission, and was overseeing it from his home in Kissimmee, Florida.

I learned that Haiti is the poorest country in the Western Hemisphere and the third poorest in the world. Its people are descendants of slaves brought from West Africa. More than two hundred years ago its people staged an uprising and dedicated their country to Satan in exchange for independence from France. They got their independence, but have been in bondage to Satan ever since. Though most Haitians are nominally Christian, Voodoo pervades every part of their lives. Voodoo keeps them destitute and deprived of hope and opportunity. Crime and corruption keep the country deprived of infrastructure and basic services such as health care and education.

During the year that Yvan lived in my home, divine appointments began happening in my kitchen and living room as he shared his burden with my friends and family. One friend, Mel Coil, became the ICDM board chairman and Michiana area representative. Verna became coordinator of the Hope for Haiti mission team, which has made three trips to Haiti, and Phil is a building consultant for ICDM. Carol birthed a project called "Threads of Hope for Haiti" and another that provides "Packets for Pastors." Each packet contains a nice white shirt, two neckties, two handkerchiefs and socks. Many other friends in Indiana, Michigan, Ohio, Kentucky, Florida and New Jersey have joined in ICDM's outreach to Haiti, as child sponsors, donors and mission team members.

Evangelism Resources, based in Wilmore, collaborates with ICDM to bring leadership and evangelism training to pastors and lay leaders in Haiti and other Caribbean islands. I spent Thanksgiving week in 2005 on the Colombian island of San Andres, participating in the graduation of 90 leaders who had completed this training.

When the women of the Wakarusa Missionary Church reached out seventy years ago to the new family in town, they had no idea how God would use them to change the course of a shy little girl's life and her whole family. They didn't know that that little girl would grow up to touch lives from all over the world. They would be as amazed as I am to see how God has directed that little girl throughout her life, preparing her at each stage for the next step.

I have learned that wherever I am is my mission field. Wherever I am, God has work for me to do. Each one of us is a unique work of art, created and prepared by God for a special purpose, to do the work that he has prepared for us to do. *"For we are God's workmanship, created in Christ Jesus to do good works, which God prepared in advance for us to do"* (Ephesians 2:10).

≈ 35 ≈

Remnants

The wind was picking up. The unusual calm that had marked a quiet Sunday afternoon in the park changed to an ominous foreboding. The strange golden luminosity of the spring sky turned to muddy gray. From the southwest a fast-moving black cloud appeared.

Absorbed in the book I was reading, I shivered as a cool breeze brushed my bare arms. I looked up and noticed the sudden change in the afternoon's demeanor. Spring warmth had given way to a sudden chill. I shivered again, stood up, picked up my blanket, and headed home.

Rain began falling before I could reach my apartment three blocks away. Huge drops bounced and splattered on the warm sidewalk. Before I reached my front porch, the drops became a downpour. From the porch I watched the lightning flashes and listened to the thunder reverberating across the heavens.

An hour later the rain subsided. The storm seemed to be over. Maree and I changed clothes and drove to church for the evening service.

During the second hymn we heard the wind and rain picking up in intensity. Rain and hail pounded the windows and banged on the roof. The lights went out. In the inky blackness the congregation stopped singing and listened to a roar such as most of us had never heard. Some said it sounded like a train rumbling overhead. Murmurs of fear ran through the congregation. What was happening? Was the storm going to take the roof off the church?

Pastor Gordon Bacon didn't know what was happening either, but he knew what to do. Over the noise of the storm he boomed, "Let us pray!" The sound system had died along with the lights, but Pastor Bacon prayed in a voice that both God and we were able to hear. He confessed the fear and apprehension we were feeling. He expressed confidence that God was in control of the storm. He asked protection for the people gathered in this place, and for everyone in the storm's path. He thanked God for hearing the prayers of his people and for promising never to leave or forsake us.

The roar passed, but the rain continued. Sirens wailed throughout the city. We stayed where we were, and waited for the lights to come back on.

In the dark sanctuary the song leader led us in singing "A Shelter in the Time of Storm." Without electrical power the organ was silent, but the piano was not. We sang our confidence and reliance on the Lord. Hymn after hymn we sang, until the lights flickered twice and then came on to stay. We blinked at the brightness as the sanctuary filled with light

Maree and I left the church and headed home. On our way, we saw evidences of the storm everywhere: flooded streets, tree limbs down, stately trees fallen to their death, streets and yards littered with debris. Some people headed home from church that night and found their homes gone, with nothing left but the foundation. Whole neighborhoods were destroyed in some places. A trailer park in Dunlap was wiped out. Unknown numbers of people were dead or missing.

Later we learned that a pair of tornadoes had passed on the south side of Elkhart, striking numerous towns and villages on its way across Northern Indiana. A spectacular photograph of the twin twisters filled the front page of Monday's newspaper.

The Palm Sunday tornadoes of 1965 mowed through fields and forests, leaving parallel paths of destruction that marred the landscape for years. Its remnants littered the countryside. Parts of houses, barns, cars and furniture landed miles away, caught in trees and fences or dropped into open fields. Personal possessions vanished, never to be seen again.

The day after the storm, President Lyndon Johnson visited the area to view the devastation. He pronounced Northern Indiana a disaster area and promised emergency funds to help with rebuilding. Churches and service organizations, friends and neighbors rallied to the aid of stricken neighborhoods, providing emergency shelter, food and clothing, and helping with the enormous tasks of cleanup.

I heard that friends of mine had lost their home and all its contents. They had nothing left except the clothes they were wearing and the car they drove to church that Palm Sunday night. Had they been at home instead of in church, they would have lost their lives too. I drove to the place where Dick and Charlotte's home had been, and saw nothing but a cement slab. In one corner sat a Rubbermaid dishpan holding all they could find of their belongings.

I looked at the dishpan holding the remnants of their lives and cried.

$\approx$ 36 $\approx$

Camping

I have tent-camped across the United States from north to south and east to west. As a single woman I camped with single-women friends, visiting state and national parks and experiencing the wonders of our great land. Later I camped with Bill and Jimmy at Rolling J Ranch and in campgrounds across the country from Los Angeles to Indiana and back.

One summer my roommate Maree, her sister Rachel and I visited Gettysburg, Washington, D.C., Virginia, West Virginia and Ohio. In Fairfax, Virginia, we found a spot in a lovely campground, pitched our tent and decided to go swimming in the Olympic-size pool before finishing our camp setup.

We had been in the water only a few minutes when a voice blared over the loudspeakers, "Everyone out of the pool! Now!" We obeyed immediately, but heavy rain pelted us even before we could get out. Lightning flashed, thunder rolled, and gale-force wind nearly blew us over as we made our way back to our campsite.

We took refuge in my 1955 Chevy and shivered in our wet swimsuits and towels. While waiting for the storm to let up, we dined on peanut butter sandwiches, boiled eggs, veggie sticks and fruit.

Our tent collapsed in the storm and was filled with water. A kind man camping next to us with his family helped us get the tent upright, stakes firmly reset and ropes tightened. After helping us bail the water out of the tent, our Good Samaritan unrolled a sheet of heavy plastic for the tent floor to keep our sleeping bags dry. Thank goodness they were still in the car when the storm came.

Tucked in at last for the night, we listened to the rain's continuing patter and fervently hoped we would not have to make a trip to the bathroom before morning.

After all these years I still have that big sheet of plastic and use it to help me in my gardening tasks. It brings back memories of an adventure in camping, and a total stranger's kindness.

⇒ 37 ⇐

My (Almost) Perfect Wedding Day

Pasadena, California, June 6, 1969 – Tomorrow is my forty-first birthday, *and* my wedding day. I'm going to be married at four p.m. It's eleven-thirty now, and time to get some sleep – if I can.

Today has been a hectic day, tending to details to make my wedding day perfect.

First I drove to Los Angeles International Airport to pick up Mama and Daddy, Carol and Verna, flying in from Indiana. Next I took Carol and Verna to the bridal shop to be fitted with rental dresses, then back to the shop to pick up the dresses when they were ready.

While I drove them from place to place, they drove me crazy with their ridiculous behavior and silly laughter. They seem to have some kind of secret between them, and I have no clue what it is. They acted like a couple of country hicks in the big city.

I picked up my wedding gown from Henshey's Department Store and took it to the church to hang overnight in the room where I'll get dressed. After settling my sisters and parents into their motel rooms I came back to my apartment, did my nails, and checked to make sure I hadn't forgotten anything. Tomorrow will be a full day, with hair appointments and rehearsal in the morning, rehearsal luncheon, wedding cake and flower deliveries—and then the wedding and reception.

Now I'm finally ready for bed and some rest. As I'm trying to relax, the phone rings. It's Arden calling from the Huntington Hotel in nearby

Arcadia. He's just flown in from Minneapolis, has taken a shuttle bus to the Huntington, and needs a ride to the motel where Mama, Daddy, Carol and Verna are staying. He hasn't bothered to tell me he's coming, so I have not made reservations for him.

I drive to the Huntington and ferry him to the motel, return to my apartment and climb into bed again. By now it's one a.m.

At one-thirty the phone rings again. It's Arden. He has to meet someone at the train station in Los Angeles and could he borrow my car. At this point my roommate Kae pokes her head in my bedroom to intervene. She tells me in no uncertain terms that I need to get some sleep. She will take care of the car business.

The person Arden is picking up turns out to be Uncle Harve, who has ridden a train all the way from Indiana to attend my wedding. I didn't know *he* was coming either. He is the secret my sisters were giggling about all day as they stroked imaginary Amish beards.

Does anyone sleep on the night before her wedding? Even without such interruptions?

Saturday, June 7, 1969 – My wedding day dawns gray and foggy and remains so for most of the day, which is not unusual for Pasadena in June. I determine not to let it dampen my happiness. This is a day to be savored and enjoyed. Our wedding will be in Hutchins Chapel at Lake Avenue Congregational Church, where Bill and I met in the single adult group almost two years ago.

Today is also my birthday. At our ten a.m. rehearsal Bill gives me a birthday card that says on the front, "I'm giving you something special for your birthday." Inside is a grinning guy saying "ME!" It's signed, "Love, Bill." Then he gives me the beautiful double-strand pearl necklace we've picked out together to wear with my ivory wedding gown.

In the bride's room Kae finds my beautiful wedding gown in a heap on the floor. Without missing a beat, she takes it back to Henshey's to be pressed again. It looks perfect when I arrive to get dressed. She doesn't tell me about the episode until later.

At four p.m. I'm standing with Mama and Daddy in the room at the back of the chapel, waiting for Mama to be ushered to her seat. Verna and Carol will proceed down the aisle next, and then will come the cue for Daddy to walk me down the aisle.

Daddy looks at me with tears in his eyes and says in a choked-up voice, "Daughter, this is the happiest day of my life." Since I am his firstborn child and the last one to get married, he must have wondered many times whether this day would ever come. Later I learn that his declaration offended Mama. She wanted *their* wedding day, more than forty years ago, to be the happiest day of his life.

Now the organ is playing *Jesu, Joy of Man's Desiring,* and I am walking down the aisle on Daddy's arm. I see Bill waiting at the front, with his brother Stan as best man and brother Richard as groomsman.

"Who gives this woman to be married to this man?" asks John Jacobs, the minister who has done our premarital counseling.

"Her mother and I," says Daddy as he places my hand in the hand of my waiting groom.

At age forty-one I am finally getting married. Bill McMillan is a man worth waiting for, and this is the day I've been waiting for all of my life.

Though I want to remember every detail of the ceremony, it goes by in a blur. Then I hear Pastor Ray Ortlund saying, "You may kiss your bride." Bill does so with gusto, and I kiss him back. We hold each other tight in our first embrace as husband and wife.

During the reception, Bill's young niece and nephew, Leslie Ellen and Marlin, make frequent trips to the refreshment table and deplete the supply of mints and nuts.

Many people we had expected at the reception don't show up. We learn later that as they waited to ride the elevator up to the Sky Room for the reception they saw us going down the other elevator to get photos taken. Assuming we are already leaving on our honeymoon, they skip the reception.

The wrong people catch the bouquet and the garter. The top layer of the wedding cake and all the leftover cake disappear after the reception, and no one knows what happened to them. Another thing Kae doesn't tell me about until later.

We never do find out what happened to the top layer, which Kae and Loretta had planned to freeze for us to enjoy on our first anniversary. The rest of the cake has gone with Bill's sister Ruth to the family gathering at his mother's house.

After changing into traveling clothes for our trip to Santa Barbara, we expect many of our friends to follow us with horns blaring, but they have already left to go out together for the evening. Bill is disappointed to find no tin cans, old shoes, streamers or "Just Married" signs on his 1965 silver gray Buick Riviera—now *our* Riviera.

The only car that follows us with its horn honking is the one carrying Gloria and her children, with their bellies now full of mints and nuts. Gloria's husband, Les, had something more important to do on our wedding day, which is also his and Gloria's anniversary. Gloria makes a plucky attempt at belling the newlyweds, but no heads turn and no one waves and smiles at us as we make our way toward the Santa Monica Freeway.

We stop for dinner at the Penguin Restaurant in Santa Monica, where our waitress is delighted to learn we've just been married. She tops off her excellent service with a complimentary slice of cake for the newlyweds and "Congratulations" written on the check.

Our destination is the beautiful Santa Barbara Inn on the beachfront. It is everything that Stan has said it would be, an idyllic place to spend our honeymoon. We open the ribbon-tied box that Kae and Loretta have prepared for us. Inside we find wedding cake – and mints and nuts. We call room service and order coffee.

Our almost-perfect wedding day is over. Our new life is about to begin. But that's another story.

Bill and Shirley, newlyweds, 1969

38

Instant Parents

I was forty-one and Bill almost forty-two when we married, too old (we thought) to begin having babies. If we were to have a family, we would need to adopt, but we were not in a hurry. Before launching into parenthood we needed time to enjoy being married.

We each taught a children's Sunday school class, and both of us were busy with other church ministries. I felt fulfilled in my work as public relations coordinator for the Children's Baptist Home of Southern California, a residential treatment center for emotionally disturbed children. My work was helping to facilitate a ministry to ninety children and teens. Perhaps this was my calling.

Two and a half years went by. Then came the news the last week of January that Verna's husband, Jack Harrington, had died. Bill and I flew to Indiana for the funeral. When we returned to Los Angeles on January 31, we had with us my nephew Jimmy and a consent-to-adopt document.

Jimmy, Howard's second son, had never known his birth mother, who died when he was four months old and Odell a year and a half. Sonja had cared for the brothers for two years, until she had to relinquish them because of health problems. For the next year, Jimmy and Odell were shuttled from place to place: two weeks with Grandpa and Grandma, two weeks with Carol and Gene, two weeks with Verna and Jack. Then Howard moved into a mobile home in Wakarusa so he could have his sons with him and they could still spend time with their grandparents and aunts.

After Jack's burial we returned to Verna's house and sat down to a table loaded with food that friends and neighbors had brought in. Five-year-old Jimmy, bewildered and upset by the events of the past few days, looked at the food on his plate and said he wasn't hungry. When this brought a demand that he eat what was on his plate, Sonja spoke up for Jimmy.

Suddenly no one was hungry. All the adults except Verna went to Howard's place for a family council meeting. Family members aired their concerns for Jimmy's emotional and physical well being. Sonja pleaded with Howard to seek professional counseling for Jimmy and himself. Howard listened to what each one had to say. Then he spoke.

"I've tried, and I've failed," he said, then announced that he was prepared to give custody of Jimmy to any couple in the room that would be willing to take him permanently.

Bill and I offered, and Howard accepted. We took Jimmy with us to Los Angeles three days later and became instant parents.

Jimmy, age 4

39

Jimmy Sings

Jimmy has been singing since early childhood. When he came to us at age five he began to bless us with songs he knew from church and Sunday school and VBS. He sang them morning, noon and night. On car trips his sweet boy-soprano voice blessed us from the back seat. He sang Bible verses to tunes he made up. He made up words and tunes to sing his own thoughts and experiences.

At church he sang solo parts in children's musicals. At school he was chosen to sing in a citywide children's choir in the Dorothy Chandler Pavilion at the Los Angeles County Music Center.

As his teen years approached, Jimmy worried about his voice changing from high to low and that he would never be able to sing high again. It didn't happen. He acquired a beautiful lyrical tenor voice, and now sings both tenor and baritone, and sometimes bass when necessary.

From early on, Jimmy wanted to pursue a career in Christian music.

"It's all I ever wanted to do," he says.

He's been traveling and singing Southern Gospel full time for nine years. With groups such as the Heartland Boys, the Wilburns and the Toney Brothers he has sung at the National Quartet Convention, Jubilee at Sea cruises and Gaither video tapings.

For Jimmy, Gospel music is about ministry, not entertainment, and his favorite place to minister is the local church.

"Up close and personal where you can see the Lord working," he says. And he has ministered in churches across the U.S. from coast to coast and north to south.

This year he launched his own group called McMillan and Life (on the Web at Mcmillanandlife.com).

Jimmy began writing song lyrics while still in his teens, and has many songs to his credit, recorded by numerous artists. He's always looking for the next song idea, he says – in a sermon, a friendly conversation, or even in special times of need.

When it came to choosing an email screen name, <u>Jimmysings</u> was a natural, for that is what he does. Jimmy sings.

Jimmy sings, 2007

≈ 40 ≈

A Strong Hand Took the Wheel

It happened on our way home from a family fun night at our church in West Los Angeles. We had just turned right from Centinela onto Rose Avenue and were moving at minimal speed. An approaching car came up the hill, zigzagged across the center line without slowing down, and headed straight for our little Toyota Corolla. It was going to hit us head-on!

Bill was driving and I was in the front passenger seat. The back seat was filled with precious cargo: our son Jimmy, and Christoff and Katrina, the young son and daughter of our missionary friends David and Diana Weber.

As the bigger oncoming car continued its path toward us, Bill pulled a hard right on the steering wheel. We came to a stop at the curb, thankful to have avoided a head-on collision. The other car had side-swiped us on the left, leaving our little Toyota scraped and ripped from front to back. All of us were badly shaken, and the children were crying from fright, but none of us had serious injuries.

The other driver, obviously impaired before the crash, managed to get out of his car and stagger toward us. He reeked of alcohol. The police arrived to investigate the accident and arrested him for driving under the influence and for driving with a suspended license.

We drove the remaining few blocks to our home, grateful that the children had not been injured and none of us had even a scratch. As we talked about the event later, I praised Bill for his quick thinking and skillful action in avoiding a head-on collision that had seemed inevitable.

"Oh," he said, "I didn't do that by myself. It was as if a strong hand took the wheel and moved us out of that car's path!"

Both of us were awestruck and thankful for the strong hand of our guardian angel that night. And both of us recalled many times when a powerful hand had saved us from imminent peril.

Bill remembered that as a pre-teen boy in Los Angeles, he was riding his old coaster-brake bicycle on a downhill street toward a busy boulevard when his bicycle chain broke. Without the chain engaged in the sprocket he could not stop, or even slow down. "Oh God, help!" he cried. At that moment the broken chain caught in his wheel spokes and brought the bike to an abrupt halt. He had no doubt that an angelic hand had intervened.

I was riding my bike to work at CTS in Elkhart when my angel intervened for me. As I made a left turn from Main Street onto Beardsley, moving with the flow of traffic and the green light, a southbound driver sped into the intersection, intending to beat the light. I applied my coaster brake hard – and stopped with my front wheel touching the car's left side door.

Seemingly unhurt, I got back on my bike and rode the rest of the way to work. An hour later I found myself crying and shaking so hard I had to leave the assembly line, and a company driver took me to a doctor for a checkup. The doctor listened to my story, read my vital signs and told me I was suffering from shock. He sent me home for the rest of the day to recover, and I returned to work the next day. Thank you, guardian angel.

⟲ 41 ⟳

Push Every Button

I was still bleary from the anesthesia when Dr. Anagol came to the recovery room and told me the news.

"I removed the lump, and it was cancer," he said. "I removed it all. I gave your husband some information for you to read, and I want to see you in my office next Tuesday."

He was gone before I could ask any questions. Not that I would have been able to ask any intelligent questions, or process the answers, in my more-asleep-than-awake condition.

I was shocked at the news of cancer, that horrible word that all of us dread hearing. Before the lumpectomy he had told me he expected to find the breast lump was benign. Now that certainty was gone, but I took comfort in the news that he had removed all of it. I had nothing more to worry about, right?

Bill left the reading materials in the waiting room, and I never saw the information that I was supposed to read. I was not ready for the news Dr. Anagol gave me in his office on Tuesday.

"I'm reasonably certain that I removed all of the cancer," he said. "But it's possible that you might still have some malignant cells. We'll need to do a modified radical mastectomy. That's a procedure where we remove the breast and some of the lymph nodes from under your arm. Before the surgery I'm scheduling you for a liver scan and a bone scan to check for evidence of cancer cells. When breast cancer metastasizes, it usually goes to the liver or the bones first. The scan results will determine your course of treatment."

Suddenly we were dealing with something much bigger and more threatening than I had thought. Now he was not sure he had "removed it all." I reeled under the impact. We canceled plans for a trip to the East Coast to see our new granddaughter, Ashli.

The scans, done on two separate days the following week, showed no cancer in my bones or liver. I would not need chemo or radiation, at least for now, but I still needed to have the mastectomy.

I began exercising to strengthen my body and vascular system for the surgery. Bill and I fell into a routine of waking up at two or three in the morning with the big C word on our minds. Unable to go back to sleep, we would get up and go walking for an hour on the track at Mark Twain Junior High School two blocks from our house. While we walked, we talked and cried and prayed.

The surgery was scheduled for June 4, Mama's birthday, and I would come home on my birthday, June 7. She flew to Los Angeles to be with me for the surgery. Jimmy, Cathie and baby Ashli flew in from Upper Darby, Pennsylvania. Caring family and praying friends at church surrounded me. Others were praying for me back in Indiana.

Paul Mast called with words of encouragement, reminding me of an incident I had all but forgotten. Back in November of 1953, when Paul and Lois Cable and I were departing for Nigeria as new missionaries, Paul and Nila Mast came to New York to see us off. (Lois and Nila are sisters.) On the ship's deck, I noticed a large button mounted on the bulkhead with the word "Push" underneath it, and wondered what it was.

"Go ahead and push it, Shirley, and see what happens," said Paul.

I pushed it – and was nearly blasted off the deck by the sound of a foghorn above our heads.

"Shirley," Paul told me now. "Push every button to beat this disease."

Dr. Anagol told me after the mastectomy that he found no cancer in the remaining breast tissue. "I also removed most of your lymph nodes and found no cancer cells," he said.

No cancer, no chemo or radiation, no hair loss or radiation sickness. Thank you, Lord.

Wilfred called with a characteristically witty word of cheer. "I'll bet you were glad to get that off your chest," he said. And indeed I was.

Women at church approached me and revealed that they'd had mastectomies years before and were living proof that breast cancer is survivable and need not be disfiguring. With a well-fitted prosthesis, no one but my husband and I would know that a breast was missing.

A good prosthesis was one button I pushed as soon as the doctor said I was healed enough to wear one.

Exercise for my affected arm was another essential button. Bill installed a pulley for me in our patio, and I worked out several times a day. In about two weeks I had full movement back in my arm.

All that was twenty-two years ago. Now I'm encouraging other women to push every button. With early detection and treatment, breast cancer is survivable, and a mastectomy will not make you less of a woman. Go ahead and get it off your chest—and push every button.

≈ 42 ≈

Grandparenting

Parenting was both a joy and a challenge. Grandparenting was sheer delight.

Jimmy's phone call from Pennsylvania told us that Ashli Marie had made her appearance on October 6, 1984 (a Saturday). We had to wait until the following May before we got to see our first grandchild, but she was definitely worth the wait. In her photos she was beautiful. In person she was enchanting. We fell hopelessly in love with her at once.

Three years later Ashli was with us in our Los Angeles home when Jimmy called from Santa Monica Hospital the morning of October 22, 1987 (a Thursday) to tell us that Chelsea Jean had arrived. We wakened Ashli, got her dressed and hurried to the hospital to see our second granddaughter. She was every bit as precious and beautiful as Ashli. Again, it was love at first sight.

Babysitting Ashli had been fun. Babysitting Ashli and Chelsea was double the fun.

Our walks in the neighborhood were treasure-hunting expeditions. We gathered seedpods, leaves, dandelions, magnolia petals, pretty stones, bugs and butterflies and caterpillars, and brought them home to show Grandpa. He never failed to ooh and aah at our discoveries.

It was his idea to get a plastic splashing pool for the backyard, and his idea to get a red "Radio Flyer" wagon to make our neighborhood excursions even more fun. In South Bend, it was his idea to join the nearby Morris Park Country Club and take the girls for swimming lessons and fun times at the pool.

Ashli was a precocious and adventurous child, learning to walk at eight months and to talk soon after that. She was still a baby when she tried with all her might to lift a three-pound dumbbell off the floor. At age four she climbed by herself to the top of a tall playground slide while Grandma watched.

Chelsea was two years old when we all moved from Los Angeles, California, to Cassopolis, Michigan. Long days strapped in her car seat were way beyond her tolerance level. At every stop for gas she cried a pitiful one-word plea, "Out! Out!"

She waited a little longer to begin talking in earnest, but when she did she spoke in full sentences. It was obvious to me that she had listened and learned how to say things right, and then decided it was time to speak for herself. In kindergarten she learned to recite the names of all the bones in the human body, from head to toe.

From Cassopolis we moved to South Bend, to a spacious ranch-style house with a basement and a big yard. Outside the back door was a massive oak tree begging for a swing to be hung from one of its big outstretched arms. Bill lost no time fulfilling its request. In the basement he rigged a pair of swings for winter fun when it was too cold and snowy to play outside.

The first time Ashli and Chelsea stayed overnight with us in South Bend, Bill and I tried to be quiet as we waited for them to wake up in the morning. Suddenly we heard a loud banging on our front door. Bill went to the door, and two policemen charged into the entry hall.

"What are you doing in here?" I demanded.

"We're answering a 911 call about some missing grandparents," they told us.

Ashli and Chelsea had been awake too, and were being just as quiet as we were. While we were in the bathroom they peeped into our bedroom, saw our empty bed and thought we had left them alone in the house. Ashli did what any intelligent six-year-old would do. She dialed 911.

At mealtime Ashli and Chelsea loved playing waitress. Donning an apron and approaching with pad and pencil, they took our orders and served our food just as they saw servers doing it in real restaurants.

Ashli and Chelsea

When they stayed overnight with us, as they often did, our bedtime ritual was to snuggle in our big bed, read from their Bible story book and ask the questions at the end of the story. Soon *they* were reading the story and asking *us* the questions. *Read-Aloud Rhymes for the Very Young* was another favorite. Its pictures and text provided hours of fun reading for all of us.

Another ritual was telling once-upon-a-time stories about when I was a little girl and about their daddy when he was a little boy.

After moving to Wilmore I loved having Ashli and Chelsea living just across the street from me. I loved having them drop in to say Hi, to have milk and cookies, or to borrow an egg or a cup of sugar. But they were no longer little girls, and the visits soon became less frequent and less spontaneous. I found out how fleeting childhood is, and how brief the grandparenting years can be.

My little granddaughters are all grown up now. As young women they are still as lovely and as loved as ever. And now I have a son-in-law to love, Ashli's husband Jerrod, and a great-grandson to love too, Chelsea's son Camden.

The blessings of grandparenting go on and on.

Camden, 10 months, 2007

PART 3

Moving On

Growing Older Is Not for Sissies

⮚ 43 ⮘

The Phone Rang

September 6, 1970. The phone rang on a Sunday morning.

Carol was on the line. Daddy was dead of a heart attack. He died in the barn while feeding his animals after church. Mama found him face down when she went to look for him after he didn't return to the house or answer when she called.

Death came instantly, said the doctor. Daddy was only sixty, but had been in failing health from heart problems and complications. He and Mama had been married forty-two years.

"I'll come as soon as I can get a flight," I told Carol. "Tell Mama I'll be there."

That afternoon I was on a plane to South Bend via Chicago.

"Call and let them know when to pick me up at the airport," I said to Bill as I boarded.

No one was there to meet me in South Bend. I waited a half hour before calling Mama's house, where I knew everyone would be gathered. Gene and Jack came for me right away. (Bill had fallen asleep and forgot to call anyone about my flight.)

"Oh, Shirley," Mama moaned from her recliner as I entered her living room.

"Oh, Mama," I said as I went to her. "I got here as quick as I could." What else was there to say?

We held Daddy's funeral at the Oak Grove Missionary Church. Rev. Orlan Golden delivered the sermon. A half-mile-long entourage followed the hearse past Daddy's little farm on Osborne Road on the way to Olive Cemetery, five miles north of Wakarusa. There we buried him near the trees on the sunset side of the cemetery.

Daddy and Mama had been married for forty-two years. Losing him was like losing a part of herself.

Thurlo and Nora, 40th anniversary, 1968

January 25, 1972. The phone rang.

"Jack Harrington is dead," said Carol. "He was hit by a train as he was crossing the railroad track beside their house. Verna heard the crash and knew it was Jack. She was the first one at the scene."

Jack was thirty-five, and Verna was a widow at thirty-two. Bill and I flew to Indiana to be with Verna and the family and mourn this tragic loss. On January 28, a below-zero day, we buried Jack in Olive Cemetery not far from Daddy.

That evening a family meeting was convened in Howard's living room to discuss his son Jimmy, who had just turned five. At the end of that meeting, Bill and I agreed to take Jimmy to live with us.

On Monday we met with Howard at an attorney's office in Goshen to have guardianship papers drawn up with a consent to adopt. That night we left on a flight from Elkhart to O'Hare and a connecting flight from Chicago to Los Angeles.

We arrived home in the wee hours of February 1. Our adventure as parents was about to begin.

June 14, 1973. The phone rang.

Arden was calling to tell us that Sonja and Norman's son Ray was dead. Struck down by a hit-run driver as he was on his way home after collecting from his paper route customers, Ray was dead on arrival at St. Joseph Hospital in Mishawaka. He was twelve years old.

Bill, Jimmy and I drove to Indiana for the funeral, stopping in New Mexico to pick up Wilfred. With three drivers taking turns at the wheel, we pushed as hard as we dared. A flat tire outside Albuquerque delayed us, and we arrived in Mishawaka three hours too late for the funeral. Ray was buried near Daddy in Olive Cemetery.

We stayed in Indiana two more weeks to attend Verna and Phil's wedding at Camp Wildwood on June 30.

December 19, 1992. The phone rang at our home in South Bend.

"Your brother is dead," said a nurse at the Americana Nursing Home in Elkhart. Wilfred had been diagnosed with incurable cancer six weeks earlier. The lung cancer, caused by a lifetime of smoking, had metastasized to his brain. He underwent surgery to relieve the pressure that was causing severe headaches, but nothing could be done to stop the killer cancer.

Wilfred became our fourth family member to be buried in Olive Cemetery.

I remembered attending a funeral at Olive Church years earlier and hearing the song, "We Are Going Down the Valley One by One."

Yes, we are, I thought now. I wonder who will be the next one to go down that valley.

July 18, 1995. The phone rang at Elkhart General Hospital.

A nurse summoned me to come and take the call in a little room next to the nurses' station. June Bails was on the line.

"Mom died a little while ago," she said. "We thought you sisters might want to come and say goodbye before they take her body away."

"We'll come right over," I said.

Carol, Verna and I had been watching at Mama's bedside for more than a week. We didn't know whether she or Sonja would reach the pearly gates first.

Diagnosed with breast cancer in the spring of 1992, Sonja had fought bravely for more than three years. She did everything possible to beat it: a mastectomy followed by repeated rounds of chemo and radiation, even a bone marrow transplant. The cancer kept advancing, to her bones, her lungs, her brain. She spent her final days in a coma, in a hospital bed at home, with her daughters at her side.

We left our vigil at Mama's bedside and went to grieve with June, Julie and Jody. Their mother, our smart, gifted and talented sister, Sonja, had been taken from us at age 54.

Sonja had planned her own funeral, a beautiful celebration held at Cedar Road Church and climaxed by trumpets playing from the balcony. She was buried in Olive Cemetery next to Ray.

March 22, 1996. The phone rang.

"Your mother passed away about 7:30 this morning," said a nurse at Rosewood Terrace nursing home in Elkhart.

"I'll come right over," I told her.

I had sat with Mama most of the previous day, reading Bible passages, singing hymns and praying. Though she could not respond, I hoped she could hear the songs and the words I spoke.

"The angels will soon be here for you," I said. "When they come for you, it's okay to go with them. You're going to see Jesus soon."

The week after Sonja's passing, Mama underwent surgery to remove an intestinal blockage. She survived the surgery, to everyone's surprise, and spent her final months in a private room at Rosewood Terrace.

We held her funeral at the Wakarusa Missionary Church and buried her beside Daddy at Olive Cemetery. Six of her grandsons served as pallbearers. Sons, grandsons, sons-in-law and other male relatives wielded shovels to fill the grave, the way the Amish do it. That's how we wanted it done for Mama. We did not want to walk away from her resting place until the burial was complete.

May 17, 1997. The phone rang. A 911 operator answered my call.

"My husband is dead," I said. "I found him in the basement. He hanged himself."

It was six o'clock on a Saturday evening, and I had just returned from a ladies retreat at Living Waters Campground. I had been away for less than twenty-four hours. At 8:30 that morning I had spoken with Bill on the phone to tell him I would be home by suppertime.

The coroner set the time of death at nine a.m. and wrote that death had come "in seconds." I had been a widow for nine hours and didn't know it.

"A clear case of suicide," said the coroner. "No need for an investigation."

"He did it cleanly," said the officer who cut the rope and lowered Bill's body onto the basement floor. "No mess for anyone to clean up." The scene shows evidence of meticulous planning, he added.

"Is there someone you can call?" asked an officer.

With my mouth as dry as cotton and my gut wrenching with diarrhea, I called Jimmy, Verna, Carol, and Pastor Banks. Soon my house was full of people.

The funeral home people came for Bill's body, and Jimmy helped carry him up the basement stairs. He made the calls to our McMillan relatives in California. He drove me to Verna's house where I would stay the next few nights. I was blessed to have my son to lean on.

We held Bill's memorial service at Gospel Center Church on May 20, and another at First Baptist Church of West Los Angeles two weeks later. In November we buried his ashes at Olive Cemetery, in a plot Verna gave me next to Jack's grave. Bill's friend and mine, Mel Coil, led the service of committal.

Some months before his death, Bill had shown me a file card with the words he wanted engraved on his tombstone. We did just as he asked. On the front are the words "Gone Home" and "Whosoever will may come." On the back is his life verse, "So whether you eat or drink or whatever you do, do it all for the glory of God" (1 Corinthians 10:31).

I don't know how his troubled mind worked, or how he thought his final act could glorify God, but he had spent a lifetime trying to live up to those words.

⇒ 44 ⇐

Mass Murder in Minnesota

"Did you hear about Arden?" Mama asked as I entered her room at Miller's Merry Manor in Wakarusa.

What a name for a nursing home. The place was anything but merry, and there was nothing merry about the patients. Feeble in body and failing in mental function, they were here to spend their final days. They knew it, and their families knew it.

I made the trip to Miller's Merry Manor once or twice a week and sometimes more. As Mama's dementia progressed, the visits grew increasingly difficult.

"What about Arden?" I asked. "I haven't heard anything."

"He murdered his whole family," she said.

"Oh my, how awful! Are you talking about my brother?"

"Yes, your brother Arden in Minnesota. He killed his whole family. There was blood everywhere."

"Where did you hear that, Mama?"

"Somebody that works here told me about it. They saw it in the paper."

"I haven't heard anything about it, Mama. I'm sure the person who told you was either mistaken or talking about someone else. Or maybe you had a bad dream."

"No, it was not a dream." She was adamant. "It was in the newspaper."

"Do you know what newspaper it was in? Did anyone show it to you?"

"No."

"I'm going to do some investigating, Mama, and I'll let you know what I find out. Now it's time to take care of your nails. Are you ready to have your fingernails and toenails done?"

"Yes," she said. I helped her move from the bed to her platform rocker.

As the focus changed to her nails, the conversation shifted too. She never mentioned the supposed mass murder again, and neither did I.

I didn't know whether it was her dementia or her medications causing her to hallucinate. Or perhaps she had heard someone talking about the real mass murder that had recently taken place on County Road 42 just east of Wakarusa.

⇒ 45 ⇐

The Thief

"Just think of what Pop and I started," Mama said one day as we talked about her dozens of grandchildren and great-grandchildren. Twenty-three grandchildren at last count, and no one knows how many great-grands.

Mama loved her grandchildren, and loved to have them come to visit. And, like most grandparents, she sometimes loved to have them go home too. She once told me that when they left after a visit, she usually waited a few days before cleaning their little handprints off her big picture window and the kitchen windows. She wanted to savor the memory of their visit. She continued to cherish their visits after she sold the farm and moved to Osceola and then to York Street in Mishawaka.

From there she continued to drive to Nappanee every week to have her hair done. That's where she was going the day an oncoming car skidded across an icy patch on the highway and hit her head-on, then spun around and hit her again on the driver's side.

Her car was totaled. A photo on the front page of the South Bend Tribune showed the crumpled front end with her "Jesus" license plate intact. The full text on the plate read, "You've got a friend in JESUS." And Mama did.

Mama suffered a broken right wrist, head injury and chest trauma. Her seat belt caused painful bruising on her chest, but saved her life. The internal bruising and jarring caused worse pain than the visible injuries. After surgery to repair her wrist, she came home with an external "fixator" to hold it in place. With therapy she regained the use of her wrist. But her loss of cognitive skills increased.

After her recovery, Mama bought another car, with the hope of driving again. She found satisfaction from seeing it in her garage and telling herself she could drive if she wanted to. We were relieved that she never did. When she wanted to go somewhere, she would ask one of us to take her in her car.

Mama's next move was to a one-bedroom apartment at Tanglewood Trace, a senior living facility in Mishawaka. Then came repeated unexplained falling, each event causing head injuries and a visit to the emergency room. It became obvious that she needed more care than any of us could give her in our homes. A private room at Miller's Merry Manor in Wakarusa was the answer. We furnished it with some of her familiar furniture to make it as homey as possible.

Over the next year and a half, we watched in dismay as dementia stole away the Mama we knew. She could still play spelling games and her harmonica, but could not remember what we had spoken of moments before. Sometimes she didn't recognize us when we came to visit. Dementia took away her precious memories of people she loved. One day she asked plaintively, "Do you remember what my mother looked like?" Another time, "Do you remember what Pop looked like?" Dementia took away her sense of propriety in speech and behavior. She said things she would have washed our mouths out with soap for saying.

In July of 1995 Mama went to Elkhart General Hospital with a bowel obstruction caused by scarring from her gall bladder surgery thirty years earlier. Absolutely nothing was getting through, not even water. It all came back up, sometimes without warning, spewing out of her mouth like a foul-smelling geyser. One day she complained, "My mouth tastes like s—t." And that's exactly what it smelled like too.

In her frail and weakened condition, the doctor doubted that she could survive surgery to remove the blockage. We began a round-the-clock death vigil in her hospital room. Carol, Verna and I took turns staying with her. Verna shopped for a "going away" outfit for her to be buried in.

Sonja was on her deathbed at the same time, and we wondered who would go first. Sonja did. We left Mama's bedside and went to mourn the death of our youngest sister, the "baby" of the family.

A few days later, Mama suddenly "woke up" from whatever state she'd been in, and wondered where she was. Surprised to learn she was in Elkhart General Hospital, she asked why she was there. I told her she was very, very sick.

"Am I going to die?" she asked.

"Yes," I said. "The doctor said that without an operation you will die, but he doesn't think you can survive an operation."

"Well, if I need an operation I want it," she said.

Surgery was scheduled for the next morning, and she surprised all of us. She spent her final eight months at Rosewood Terrace in Elkhart. Death took her on March 22, 1996.

A thief named Dementia had already stolen her from us months before.

⤜ 46 ⤛

Angels in My House

It happened on a balmy spring day, May 17, when the pink azaleas in front of our house were in glorious full bloom. I'd been away overnight at a ladies' retreat and came home at five-thirty Saturday evening to a silent, empty house. It seemed strange that Bill didn't meet me at the door or answer when I called to him. I looked for him in every room. He wasn't there.

Maybe he's working outside or chatting with a neighbor, I thought. But he wasn't outside, and no one had seen him.

I found him in the basement, dead by hanging.

"A clear case of suicide," said the coroner. Time of death nine a.m., he wrote on the death certificate.

I stayed with Verna for the next few nights. After that my friend Wilma came over and slept in my guest room most nights. Sometimes I slept at her house or stayed with Carol or Verna.

A month passed, and I had not found the courage to stay alone in my house. Anxiety and dread seized me every time I came home and turned the key to open the door. I relived the awful experience over and over.

At Bill's memorial service my friend Elaine had given me a comforting word that helped me during the daytime, but I could not bear to be alone at night.

"When I heard the news of Bill's death," she said, "I saw angels there with him to carry him to heaven. And I saw angels there with you too.

You are not alone. Whenever you feel afraid or lonely, the angels are there to watch over you."

I believed it, but the anxiety persisted.

"I can't go on like this," I told my counselor one day through tears. "I'm going to sell my house and move away—anywhere to get away from the horrible memories."

"Why don't you give yourself a little time before making that decision," he suggested. His tone was warm and reassuring. "If you wait a week or two, maybe even a month or two, you may feel different about it." His advice matched that of every book I'd read on the subject.

"I'll try," I said. "I'll wait two weeks, but after that I'm going to move."

I went home from that counseling session and began to think more about the angels being there with me. I walked through the rooms, visualizing angels all around me and thanking God that they were watching over me.

I read about angels in my Bible and found accounts of them from Genesis to Revelation.

"He will command his angels concerning you to guard you in all your ways," I read in Psalm 91:11.

In mid June I tried staying alone for the first time.

"Lord, I can't do this by myself," I said. "You'll have to help me." And he did.

As I got into bed I thanked God for his angels all around me, filling every room in my house. I slept soundly and peacefully through the night, and from that night on I stayed alone.

Eventually I could even go to the basement alone. One night in July, when the weather service issued a tornado warning, I took a flashlight, a radio and my cordless phone and went to the basement for shelter until the tornado warning was lifted.

I stayed in my house for two more years before moving to Kentucky to be near my son and granddaughters. I sense the angels with me here too. Unseen but real, they watch over me whether I'm awake or asleep.

≈ 47 ≈

I Just Wanted You to Know

R-r-ring! The sound of the telephone was welcome to my ears. It was Sunday afternoon, and I was spending it alone, as I often did these days.

I was delighted to hear the voice of my granddaughter Ashli, thirteen at the time.

"Hello, Ashli," I said. "I'm so glad to hear from you. How are you?"

"Fine," she said. But she didn't sound fine.

"Grandma," she said. "I just wanted you to know I'm thinking of you."

"How nice!" I replied. "I think of you a lot. When can you and Chelsea come and stay overnight with me again? You haven't been here for awhile."

"I don't know," she said. "Well, I gotta go now. Bye."

"Bye-bye, Ashli. Thank you for calling. I love you."

"I love you too."

A brief conversation, but it meant so much to me that she had called just to say, "I'm thinking of you."

A few minutes later the phone rang again. It was Ashli.

"Grandma," she said, "my mom said I needed to call you back and tell you why I was thinking of you. Do you remember what day this is?"

I remembered. It was May 17, a whole year since Bill's suicide.

"Yes," I said. "I remember. Thank you for remembering too. And thank you for calling to tell me. That means a lot to me. We miss Grandpa so much, don't we?"

"Yes," she said, this time through tears.

"Grandpa loved you and Chelsea so much," I said. "And so do I."

"I love you too. Bye."

48

Moving Day

June 15, 1999. Moving day had arrived. I had waited two years before making this decision. Now it was time to move on.

In February I bought a mobile home in Florida, where I planned to spend winters. In April I bought a home in Wilmore, Kentucky, where Jimmy and his family now lived. Seven days later a buyer from New Jersey signed a contract to purchase my home in South Bend. In May I returned to Kentucky to close on the house in Wilmore.

Throughout the month of May I disposed of things I didn't need and would not have room for in a smaller house. Carol and Verna, Phil and Gene helped with yard sales and giveaways. Friends carried everything from furniture to firewood to tools out of the basement, and helped to empty the garage.

On June 15, with the help of a host of family members and friends, I moved to Wilmore.

And between January and my move in June I underwent two electrocardioversions to jolt my heart out of atrial fibrillation and back into rhythm. The first was in March while I was in Florida. The second was on the first of June, two weeks before moving day. It left me drained, with no strength to pack for my move. My sisters and several friends from church came and had a packing party. By the end of the day all my shelves, drawers, cupboards and closets were empty and everything was in boxes.

On June 14 a crew of men from church showed up to help load the moving van. My three brothers-in-law came too, and Norman brought his plumbing crew. Jimmy came early to pick up the rental truck. By that evening the house was empty and the truck was bulging. A few things had to be left behind with family and friends.

Next morning we pulled away from my house on Cherry Tree Lane and headed for Wilmore, Kentucky, Jimmy in the moving van and I in my car. Without a look back, I drove away from the house that held many dear memories as well as the most painful ones of my life. It was the nicest home I had ever lived in. It was a place where Bill and I had welcomed family for holiday events, friends for Bible studies, and international students for meals and get-acquainted times.

It was also the place where anxiety and depression had descended on Bill like a black cloud, morphed into manic depressive illness (aka bipolar disorder), robbed our marriage of the joy we had known, and nearly destroyed both of us. In the end, it took his life. I was glad to leave that scene behind me, though the memory would be etched in my mind forever.

When we arrived in Wilmore, Jimmy had a crew of friends lined up to move things into my new home. They were finished in about two hours, with beds set up, furniture in place, and the garage stacked high with boxes to be unpacked.

Two years passed before there was room in my garage for a car. More years have passed, and some boxes are still waiting to be opened. One day I may call for the Salvation Army to come and take it all away. If I haven't needed the things in those boxes in the last eight years, I'm not likely to need them in the next eight, or however long I may live.

I'm hoping to end my days in my cozy house on Brookwood Lane in Wilmore. Meanwhile, I'm busy sending treasures ahead in preparation for my next move. On that moving day I will leave all my stuff behind for other people to dispose of. I can hear them now as they sort through things and wonder aloud, "Why in the world did she hang onto that?"

Watching from my new mansion, I'll probably be wondering too.

☞ 49 ☜

Changes

Widowhood has brought changes that impact everything in my life.

When the car needs servicing I'm the one who has to decide where to take it. When something goes wrong and it needs repairs, I'm the one who has to evaluate the mechanic's believability. Is he proposing expensive but unnecessary repairs because I am a woman and won't know the difference?

One day I took my car to have a coolant leak repaired. The mechanic found three leaky seals, a worn rack and pinion and numerous other things that he said needed attention. The bill came to nearly $1500. Was he looking out for my welfare? Or was he taking advantage of my ignorance—and taking me for a ride?

I miss male companionship and conversation. I miss talking things over with Bill. I miss going places with him. We used to enjoy going to concerts, eating out, going to the gym together, riding bikes together, and attending church together. Going to dinner and a concert alone is no fun. Going with a female friend is better than not going at all, but it doesn't measure up to going the same places with my husband. Even the worship experience at church is altered by not having anyone to discuss it with over Sunday dinner. I used to avoid sitting in the same pew with all the other widows (widows row I called it), and I still prefer to sit in a mixed row, with a family, a young couple or an international friend.

Bill always kept the lawn meticulously mowed and trimmed. Mowing is the one thing I won't tackle. First of all, I've never mastered the art of starting a lawn mower, and second, I'd rather not walk behind a mower and breathe its nasty fumes. I know there are mowers with electric starters. I know there are electric mowers that run as quiet as a sewing machine and don't spew out carbon and lead to pollute the environment. The truth is, I don't want to walk behind a mower at all, especially in hot weather. I would rather be in my cool house working at my computer, or enjoying a tall glass of iced tea in my patio room (still in the dream stage).

Bill was a horticulturist. He knew plants by their Latin botanical names as well as the familiar ones. He would be surprised to know that I have become somewhat of a gardener myself now, and have even learned a few botanical names. I'm developing a perennial garden. I've had trees planted and landscaping done. I've learned how to prune and mulch and fertilize, and even invested in a compost tumbler to turn kitchen and yard waste into rich compost to feed my nutrient-deficient soil.

I dream of a patio room and a picture-perfect backyard filled with flowers and paths, cozy nooks with benches, and a pond with a waterfall. My dream garden will be the envy of all my neighbors. It will be on the garden tour and featured in a national home and garden magazine. The trouble with such a garden is the amount of time and work it takes to keep it looking beautiful. Sometimes I get carried away in a garden store and come home with my trunk full of flowers to plant, perennials for year-after-year beauty and annuals for instant color. Then I get busy at my computer and leave the flowers in pots, waiting to be planted, until the poor things are nearly dead.

Living in Wilmore has turned out to be one of the best changes of my life. I love the Wilmore community, the people, my church and my home. Most of all I love being near my granddaughters, Ashli and Chelsea, and now my great-grandson, Camden. They are my reason for being here—or for being anywhere, for that matter.

Chelsea, Camden and Ashli, June 2007

I've come to see that life has always involved changes. The first and biggest change was one I don't remember—the change from the safe, protected environment of the womb to life outside. Then came the change from infancy to toddlerhood, from a horizontal position to sitting and crawling and then standing upright, seeing the world in a whole new way, becoming more mobile, and a tiny bit less dependent. At six came the big change of going to school and learning to read and write, a revolutionary change that opened a whole world of information and knowledge and possibilities.

Life changes in me and in the world around me continued without letup: puberty, graduation from high school, finding a job, going to college, pursuing a call to mission, career, marriage, parenting, letting go, home ownership, grandparenting, menopause, mastectomy, retirement, knee replacement, bereavement, buying and selling a home on my own.

There will be more changes, I know—some good, some painful. Aging will always be a reality, no matter how I try to ward it off.

When is a person old anyway? The line between young and old keeps moving. When I was twenty I thought twenty-five was old. At forty I thought sixty was old. At sixty I thought eighty was old. Now that I'm nearly eighty, the marker has moved further still. Will I be old at ninety? At one hundred? The answer will largely have to do with how much mobility and independence I can maintain. To maintain these as long as possible, I try to exercise on my stationary bike most days of the week. The key word here is "try," for other, more urgent, things often preempt my good intentions.

One change has come that I didn't expect. Life is better now than I ever thought it could be, and one of the best things is time. If I want to stay up and write half the night, or the whole night, no one objects. In that sense I have more time than ever before. Yet, as the used-up part of my life increases, the time I have left diminishes and time becomes more and more precious.

The latest changes in my life won't be the last. This stage, like each one before it, is preparing me for the next. Change is the one constant in this journey from birth to death, and into the exciting new life beyond.

$\Longrightarrow$ 50 $\Longleftarrow$

Waiting at the Bus Station

Waiting at the bus station on the north side of Lexington, I wonder: "How will I recognize him? I know he's black, but everyone in this place is black. I'm the only fair-skinned person here."

I carry a small sign that says ASBURY SEMINARY, hastily lettered with black Magic Marker on a manila folder.

There hasn't been time to exchange photographs or letters. The man I'm to meet is a Haitian-born pastor who lives in Florida with his wife and three children, and he's coming to Wilmore, Kentucky to do his final year of seminary at Asbury.

Just six days ago I read a small notice in the church bulletin that said a pastor from Florida needs a private home where he can receive room and board for the fall semester. "If you can help, please call this number." Immediately I felt impressed to call.

When Steve answered my call on Monday morning and told me the pastor is from Haiti, I knew why I was supposed to call. Here was an opportunity to offer hospitality to an international.

Bill and I had loved extending friendship and hospitality to international students in Los Angeles and in South Bend, and I was already reaching out to internationals in Wilmore. I helped some of them with written and conversational English. I invited them for meals in my home. I carried business cards identifying me as an "international friendship specialist." But I hadn't planned to have internationals living with me in Wilmore.

171

"The pastor's name is Yvan Pierre," said Steve, "and he's from Haiti. He can't afford to live on campus and has asked us to help him find room and board in a private home."

My heart warmed, and I told Steve that I might be interested in taking in this student.

"I have to tell you that he's black," said Steve.

"His skin color is not important," I replied, "as long as he's a brother in the Lord."

Steve gave me Yvan's phone number in Florida, and I gave Steve permission to give Yvan my phone number. I would wait for him to call me.

Meanwhile, I checked out the seminary's rates for on-campus housing and meals, did some figuring and decided that I could offer room and board for half that amount. When Yvan called on Tuesday, we agreed on a rate, and the following Saturday I was at the bus station waiting to meet him after his long ride from Orlando.

He was the last person to emerge from the bus. He looked exhausted, but flashed a smile as bright as summer sunshine when he saw my sign.

"Are you Yvan Pierre?" I asked.

"Yes," he said. "Are you Mrs. Shirley? You look just like I thought you would!"

"And you look like I thought *you* would too." I said with a welcoming embrace.

A special friendship began that day and grew during the next few months. His three precious children began calling me Grandma Shirley. In May the whole family spent graduation week in my home: his wife Miriam, daughters Gemima and Gaina, and son Jesse. I grieved with him when his father died soon after Yvan arrived in Wilmore. His father had also been his best friend, mentor and role model.

Answering that notice in the church bulletin changed my life and opened new opportunities for ministry. I have stayed many times in the Pierres' home in Kissimmee, Florida. I have gone with Yvan on mission trips to the area where he grew up in Haiti. I met and fell in love with his mother, brothers and sisters, most of whom are involved in the ministry of the International Christian Development Mission (ICDM), which Yvan founded and directs.

In Haiti I saw a land of desperate need and dire poverty, a land where children get sick and die because of malnutrition, where women and their babies die in childbirth without ever seeing a doctor, where every waking moment is consumed with trying to feed their families. I saw a people without hope.

I saw children being offered hope and a future through education and spiritual nurture. I saw bright young people who are now in high school and trade schools, being equipped for a better life than their parents ever dreamed of. I met pastors whose passion is to spread the good news of Jesus to people who have been in bondage to Voodoo all their lives. I returned from those trips with Haiti in my heart, determined to return there at every opportunity for as long as I am able.

When I met that bus in Lexington that day, it brought more than the passenger I'd never met. It brought me a busload of opportunities I never expected.

≈ 51 ≈

I've Been Converted – Over and Over

My first conversion happened on a Sunday morning in August the summer I turned eight. That morning we all got dressed for church as usual, but instead of going to church in town we went to camp meeting six miles away. We'd never been to camp meeting before and didn't know what to expect.

People came from all over the district to gather in the big tabernacle and listen to Bible teaching and preaching. I went to the children's tabernacle, where we sang songs and heard a Bible story. When the story lady invited us to come and pray to receive Jesus as Savior, I hurried forward. I knew that I was a sinner, and I couldn't wait to have my sins forgiven. Afterward I couldn't wait to tell Mama what had happened.

That morning my life was changed forever.

Now fast-forward more than fifty years. After a family picnic on Santa Monica Beach my heart suddenly began racing wildly, out of rhythm. I was so weak and sweaty and short of breath I could barely make it across the sandy beach.

Next day our family doctor told me I was experiencing atrial fibrillation. He prescribed a medicine to strengthen and slow the beats. A few days later I felt a sudden intense pounding, as if my heart was going to jump out of my chest, then a return to quiet, steady rhythm.

That was my first medical conversion to "sinus rhythm." Over the years since then I experienced more episodes of "a fib" and more conversions.

Then came my first electric cardioversion in 1997. Arrhythmia had persisted for weeks without responding to medication. I needed to be converted with a defibrillator, the paddle device we've seen doctors and paramedics use on television shows to restart a stopped heart. In cardioversion, electric current is used to stop the heart and then restart it in sinus rhythm. It was a little scary to think about.

First I needed to take an anti-coagulant for six weeks to minimize the risk of having a stroke. My cardiologist explained that clots can form in the heart chambers during a fib and be thrown to the brain at the time of conversion.

On the morning of May 8, 1997, Bill took me to St. Joseph Hospital in South Bend for the outpatient procedure. In the conversion room I went to sleep under low-level anesthesia and woke up a little later with my heart in perfect rhythm. I was tired and sleepy for the next few days, but felt no other side effects

Over the next ten years I've had uncounted medical conversions and three more electric cardioversions. I take prescription medicines every day, exercise on my stationary bike, and avoid stress as much as possible, a combination that works pretty well at keeping me in rhythm. Occasionally I can halt an episode of a fib by deep coughing (self CPR), then resting quietly and breathing deeply.

I'm grateful for medicines and technology to convert my heart and help it stay in rhythm, but even more grateful for that first conversion on a long-ago Sunday morning at camp meeting. That one has lasted a lifetime.

⇒ 52 ⇐

Bluebirds

It was a blue-sky day in September when I first saw them. Out of the blue, a pair of bluebirds appeared in my backyard. I had never, ever seen a bluebird, but these birds were blue, and they were not blue jays. Flashes of blue showed on their wings, backs and tails, and a rosy blush on their breasts as they flitted from the power lines to my autumn purple ash tree and back to the power lines.

I opened my *Peterson's Guide to Eastern Birds* and turned to "bluebirds." There was no doubt now. They were eastern bluebirds, and they were house hunting in my back yard. They showed a special interest in one of the two birdhouses hanging in the ash tree. They inspected the rustic brown wren house and decided it didn't suit, but several times a day they returned to look at the ceramic house fashioned to look like a basket of strawberries.

I rushed out to Walmart and bought a copy of the *Bluebird Landlord's Handbook* and two special bluebird houses constructed of red cedar, then to Lowe's to get two ten-foot mounting poles. I read all about being a good bluebird landlord, where and how to place the houses, how to protect the birds from predators, how to monitor and care for the houses. I was eager to welcome my new tenants.

Unfortunately, I was not able to set the mounting poles in the hard clay ground, and no one was available to do it for me. The poles and the houses remained in my garden shed.

The bluebirds didn't mind, however. In the spring they were back, hanging around the strawberry basket, and then making hundreds of trips a day bringing materials to furnish their home. After a while, only one of the pair was making flights: the male, bringing food for his mate, who was now a stay-at-home mom incubating her eggs.

And then the babies hatched. How many, I never found out. One day I discovered a lovely blue eggshell on the ground under the nest, and soon the flights increased as both parents came and went from dawn to dusk, foraging for food and bringing it home to their family.

I couldn't wait to see those little ones emerge from their nest, but I never saw them. They must have fledged early one morning, before I was out and about, and never returned home.

Now a pair of bluebirds is hanging around my back yard again, and I'm hoping they decide to move in.

⇒ 53 ⇐

Emergency!

Hurrying to reach our destination, Bill and I were speeding along a deserted highway in wide-open country. The road was smooth and straight, with no other cars in sight for as far as we could see. No houses either.

Bill was the passenger and I was driving, as I frequently did, for he often got sleepy and asked me to take the wheel. I was driving fast because we needed to reach our destination as quickly as possible.

It was good to be together again after such a long time, and yet I felt uneasy. In the passenger seat to my right, I could see Bill fumbling with his super-size drink in a cup without a lid. The cup slipped from his hand and the drink spilled all over the leather seat and center console and ran down onto the carpet. He grabbed a handful of tissues and tried to mop it up, but the tissues went to pieces and added to the mess.

He opened the power window and tried to throw the tissues out, along with the cup that had held the drink. Tissues and liquid went all over the car, inside and outside. Now we really had a mess on our hands.

As I instinctively reached across to help him, the car veered off the road, and the next thing I knew we were driving in tall grass that reached almost to the top of the car windows. We were still parallel to the road (I hoped) and still going fast, hardly slowing down at all.

I swerved left to get back onto the pavement. To my relief, the maneuver was successful. We were back on the road, still in the right lane and going the right direction. Our car was still the only one on the road as we continued at high speed, our destination still miles away.

Suddenly, four patrol cars appeared with lights flashing and sirens screaming. *Oh-oh,* I thought, *they're after us for littering!* I slowed to a stop with two patrol cars in front of us and two behind us. No other traffic was going in our direction, but lots of cars were now zooming by in the opposite direction.

Four officers got out and walked toward us while four others stayed in their vehicles, one in each patrol car. I rolled down my window, then opened the door at their command and prepared to step out.

Before I could get out of the car, I woke up, wondering what the strange dream meant. Why had I dreamed of Bill again after nearly eight years? Where were we going in such a hurry? To a hospital emergency room? To a doctor's appointment? To help a family member in crisis? To find help for our own crisis?

When I woke up, the emergency was over. The chaos was gone. Or was it? The fallout from Bill's suicide ten years ago continues to poison our family. I wish I could wake up and find the ongoing chaos gone. I wish I could wake up and find relationships all healed and everybody living happily ever after. That would be a dream come true.

∽ 54 ∽

Clutter

Clutter is all around me. Last year and the year before, and the year before that, I resolved to take charge and get rid of clutter. Now I find myself surrounded by more of it than ever.

A workshop leader at a writers conference said that writers work with piles, not files. That would be me, I said. And the piles continue to grow. When I run out of space on the desk and table and chairs, I start new piles on the floor.

If I try to take control, piles of paper stare at me with defiance. "What are you going to do about me?" they taunt, like rebellious teenagers beyond their parents' control.

Like a frustrated parent, I vow to put them in their place. The trouble is, I don't know where their place is. I've run out of places to pile my papers and stash my stuff.

A good friend told me that what I need to do is find a home for everything and then keep everything in its designated home. I agreed, but I have two problems. Finding a home for all this stuff takes way too much time, and I can't decide what kind of home it all needs.

What do I do with Christmas cards, birthday cards, Mother's Day cards and anniversary cards received over the years? What do I do with boxes and boxes of photographs, the record of a lifetime of events? Will anyone care about them after I'm gone? Probably not.

What do I do with piles of gorgeous magazines that whole staffs of editors and writers, artists and photographers spent months planning and producing? What do I do with reports and records and receipts that I might need to refer to sometime? What do I do with books that I've read, and might want to read again or look up a reference or a quote to use in my writing?

What do I do with outmoded equipment that I no longer use and nobody wants—an electronic typewriter, a word processor and a printer? And what about the box of framed and unframed pictures on the closet floor, and the collection of 33-rpm records? The quilting fabrics for quilts I will never make? Would more filing cabinets, bookcases and storage racks solve my problem? Or would they only become places to accumulate more stuff that I don't need? (It seems to multiply while I'm not looking.)

One wall of my garage is lined with boxes I've never opened since moving to Wilmore. I need to sort through them and decide what to give away and what to keep. But where will I put the things I want to keep? And how important can they be if I haven't looked at them in all these years? I know perfectly well that when I'm gone, none of it will matter. As Bill always said, "It's just wood, hay and stubble."

One day I surveyed the scene and mused aloud to Jimmy about my dilemma.

With the sensitivity and practicality of a man, he said, "Don't worry, Mom. It won't take me long to get rid of it when you're gone."

Thanks, Jimmy. You just took a load off my shoulders!

⟳ 55 ⟲

Shirley's Ten Tips for
Staying Young While Growing Older

1. *Think young.* Look at the world with a child's sense of wonder and curiosity. Welcome new ideas and new experiences. Explore new possibilities. Remember the past and learn from it, but don't live in it. Make the most of today, and live it to the fullest. Dream dreams and make plans for the future.

2. *Eat healthy.* Avoid foods high in fat and sugar. Eat lots of whole grains, beans, nuts, vegetables and fruits. Major on colorful fruits and vegetables packed with vitamins and minerals, flavor and eye appeal. Avoid red meat, and limit meat consumption to five ounces a day.

3. *Stay active.* Get a moderate amount of physical exercise every day. If you've been inactive, start with five minutes a day and work up to twenty or thirty minutes most days of the week. Combine exercise with pleasure. You'll be more likely to stick with activities you enjoy, whether walking, biking, dancing, swimming or gardening. Make it fun by exercising with a friend or in a group, which also adds accountability and motivation.

4. *Keep busy.* Baby-sit a grandchild. Plant and tend a garden. Enroll in a class and learn something new. Take up painting, writing, quilting, woodworking or other creative projects. Volunteer to share your skills and expertise with others. Attend lectures, concerts and programs

(many are free). Record your memories and life experiences on audio or videotape for your children and grandchildren. Write your memoirs.

5. *Get a dog.* Having a dog or other companion animal improves mental, emotional and physical health. It lowers blood pressure and heart rate and relieves stress. Walking a dog is good exercise and brings opportunities to meet people. A dog's loyalty, affection and companionship are antidotes to isolation and loneliness.

6. *Be flexible.* Keep a bag packed and ready at a moment's notice for an overnight stay with a grandchild or a trip with a friend. Be ready to interrupt your plans and take a friend to the doctor or emergency room. Be ready to drop everything when someone invites you to lunch, a concert or a shopping excursion. Better yet, initiate the activity and do the inviting.

7. *Look outward.* Look for ways to improve your neighborhood, your community and your church. Plan a block party to help neighbors get to know one another. Organize a neighborhood watch to make your neighborhood a safer place. Volunteer at your local school, community service center or church. Join a book club, a writing group or a service organization. Go on a mission trip.

8. *Keep learning.* Stretch your mind with new ideas. Exercise your mental muscles by learning new things. Enroll in a lifelong learning class. Memorize scripture or poetry. Research a new subject and become an expert on it. Build your vocabulary by looking up the meaning of new words you encounter and then using them in conversation.

9. *Reach out.* Practice seeing and loving people as individuals with needs and problems, joys and sorrows. Rejoice with those who rejoice, and cry with those who are hurting. Listen to what people say, and what they don't say. Welcome new people at church with a warm handshake and a genuine smile. (Practice smiling in front of a mirror to make sure your eyes are smiling.) Tell newcomers your name and ask theirs, and then address them by name. If a name is unfamiliar, ask how to spell and pronounce it correctly. Practice hospitality. Keep your refrigerator and pantry stocked so you can invite someone for dinner, or for tea and a snack, on the spur of the moment.

10. *Let go.* Let go of worry, anger, bitterness and resentment. Let go of disappointments, regrets, guilt and blame. Let go of the desire to control – your spouse, your teenagers, your grandchildren, your pastor,

your friends, your neighbors. Let go of things you cannot change. When you let go of these things, you let go of stress, and letting go of stress is the key to emotional and physical health. Pray the Serenity Prayer: *"Lord, give me the serenity to accept the things I cannot change, courage to change the things I can, and wisdom to know the difference."*

11. Bonus tip: *Laugh heartily.* A good belly laugh is better than any pill or potion. Laughter brings healing to both body and soul. Find something to laugh about every day. Look on the light side of life. Laugh at yourself. Read the humorous anecdotes in *Reader's Digest.* Watch a funny movie or home video. Read a funny book. Pull out all the stops and *laugh out loud.* Laughter really is the best medicine.

Laugh - It's Good Medicine!

≈ 56 ≈

Please Be Patient

When I think back over my life, I am awed by the grace of God, and by his love for me. His grace is the sweet fragrance that permeates all of my life. His grace is all the undeserved good things I've ever enjoyed. His grace helps me to make sense of the painful things that come my way.

His grace is making this present part of my life the best yet.

His grace brought me to Wilmore, Kentucky, a place I never would have thought of moving to on my own. I didn't know anyone here, except Jim and Cathie, Ashli and Chelsea. I moved to Wilmore to be near my granddaughters. I hoped to be a godly influence in their lives and help them through their teen years.

God has given me much more: a warm and deepening relationship with Jimmy, a wonderful church fellowship, new friends, and new opportunities to develop my gifts and reach out to people. He has given me a comfortable home that is just right for me at this stage in my life, with a guest room for welcoming friends and family.

In a dresser drawer I have a button from a seminar Bill and I attended long ago. It says, "PBPGINFWMY." Interpretation: "Please Be Patient. God Is Not Finished With Me Yet." I'm so glad he isn't. He is still teaching me new things and giving me new opportunities to learn and grow.

At age seventy-nine I am more contented and happy than I could ever have imagined or dreamed possible. Yet there is so much more that

I want to learn and accomplish. I'm planning to keep on learning and growing until I reach one hundred—and beyond, God willing.

So please be patient. God is not finished with me yet.

 *Not the end*

www.ingramcontent.com/pod-product-compliance
Lightning Source LLC
Chambersburg PA
CBHW031320290526
45784CB00014B/415